Unicorns Adult Coloring Book Vol 1

60 Entertaining Stress Relieving Unicorn Patterns

By Omar Johnson

Get Your Free Butterfly Mandala Coloring Book

Visit

HTTPS://WWW.ADULTCOLORINGBOOKSFORYOU.COM

Make Profits Easy LLC Publishing

omarjohnson@adultcoloringbooksforyou.com

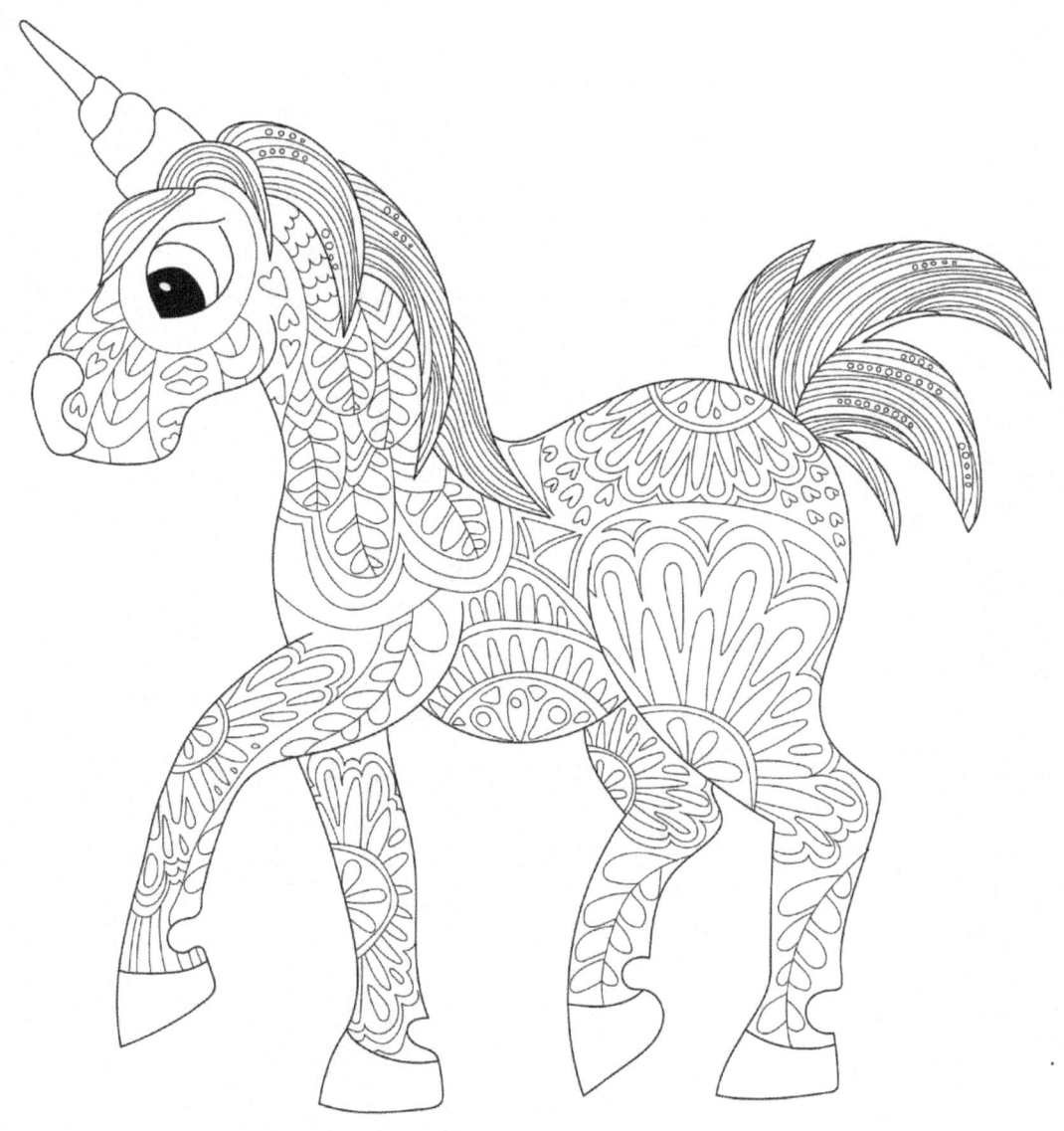

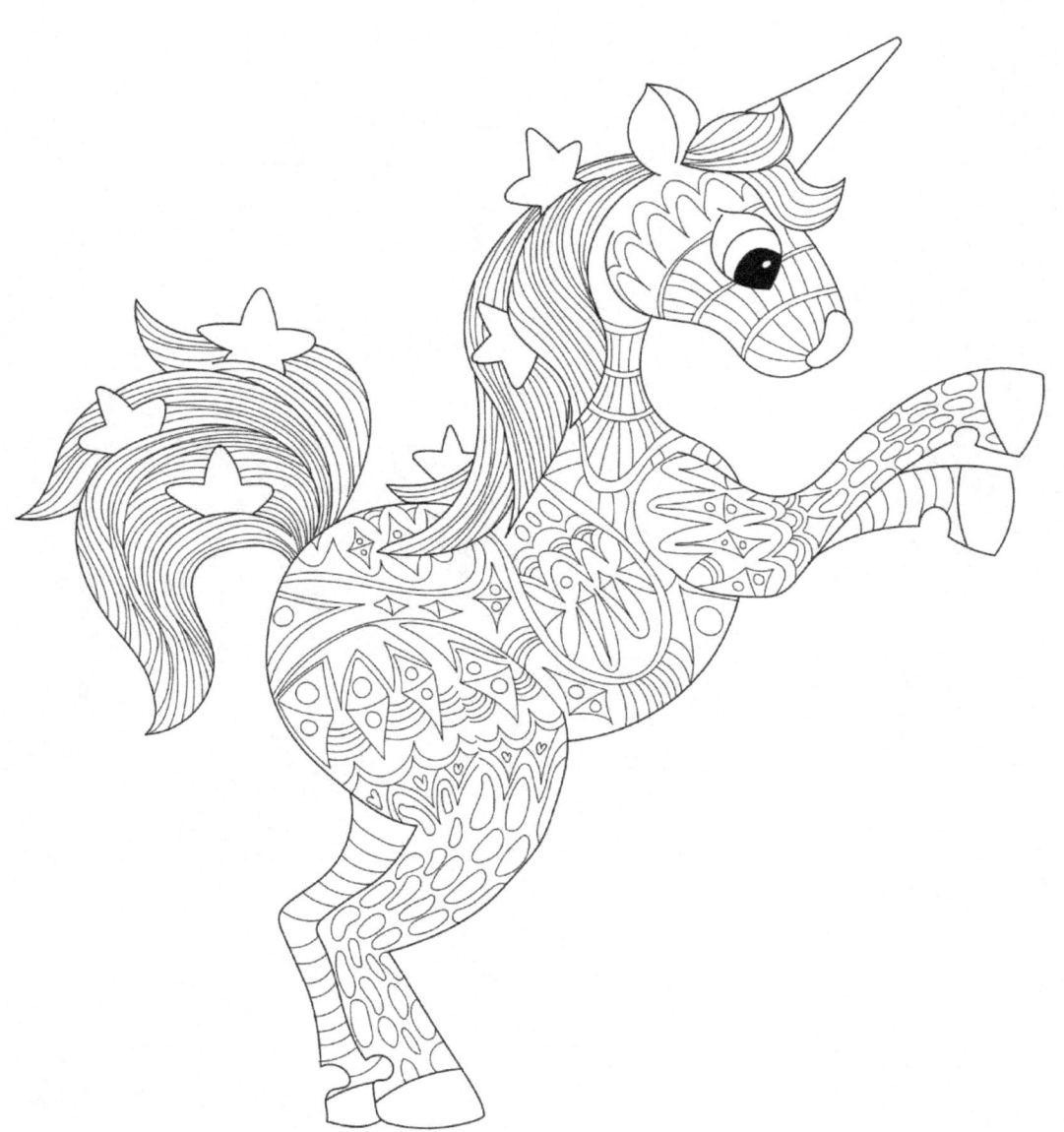

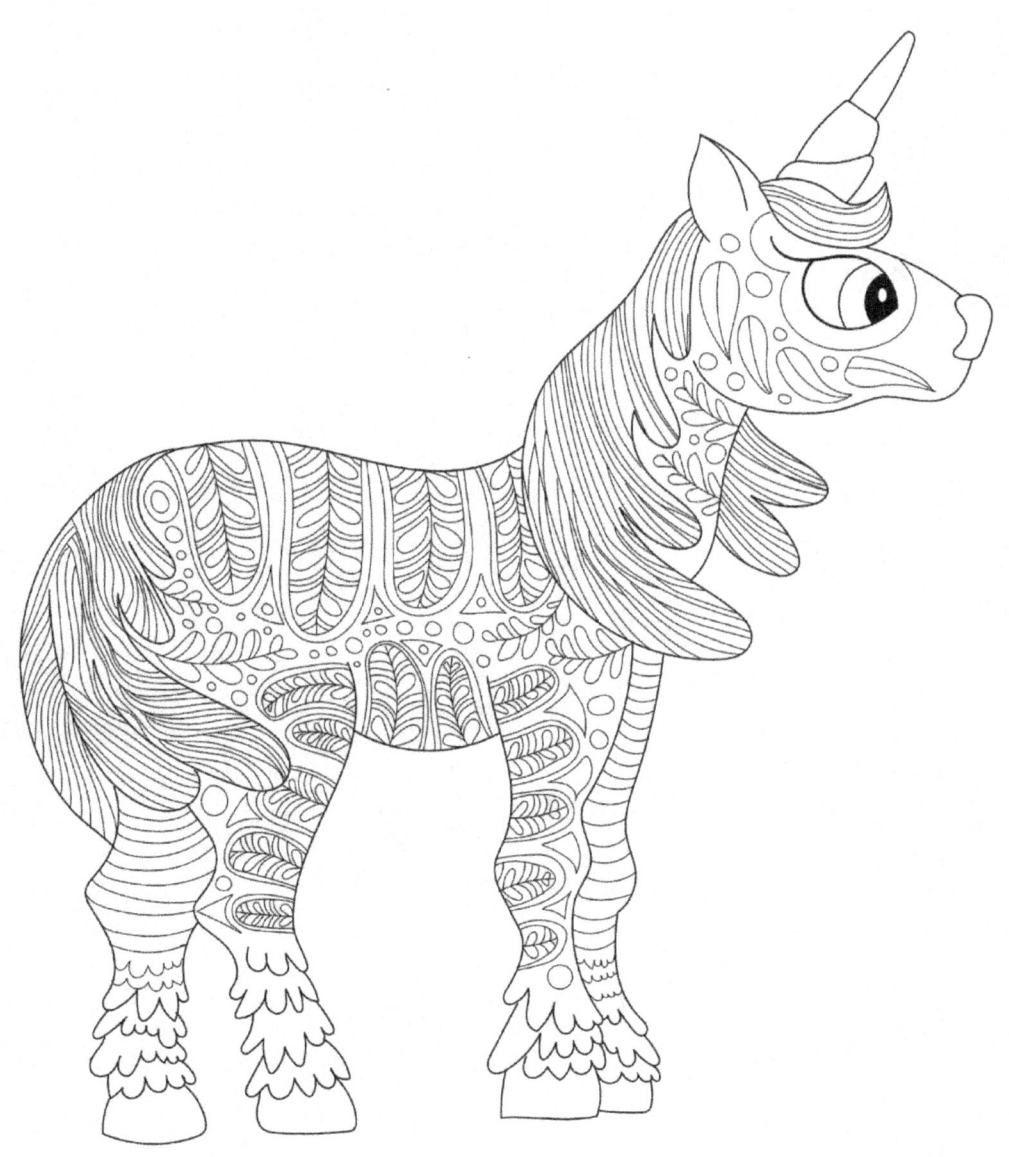

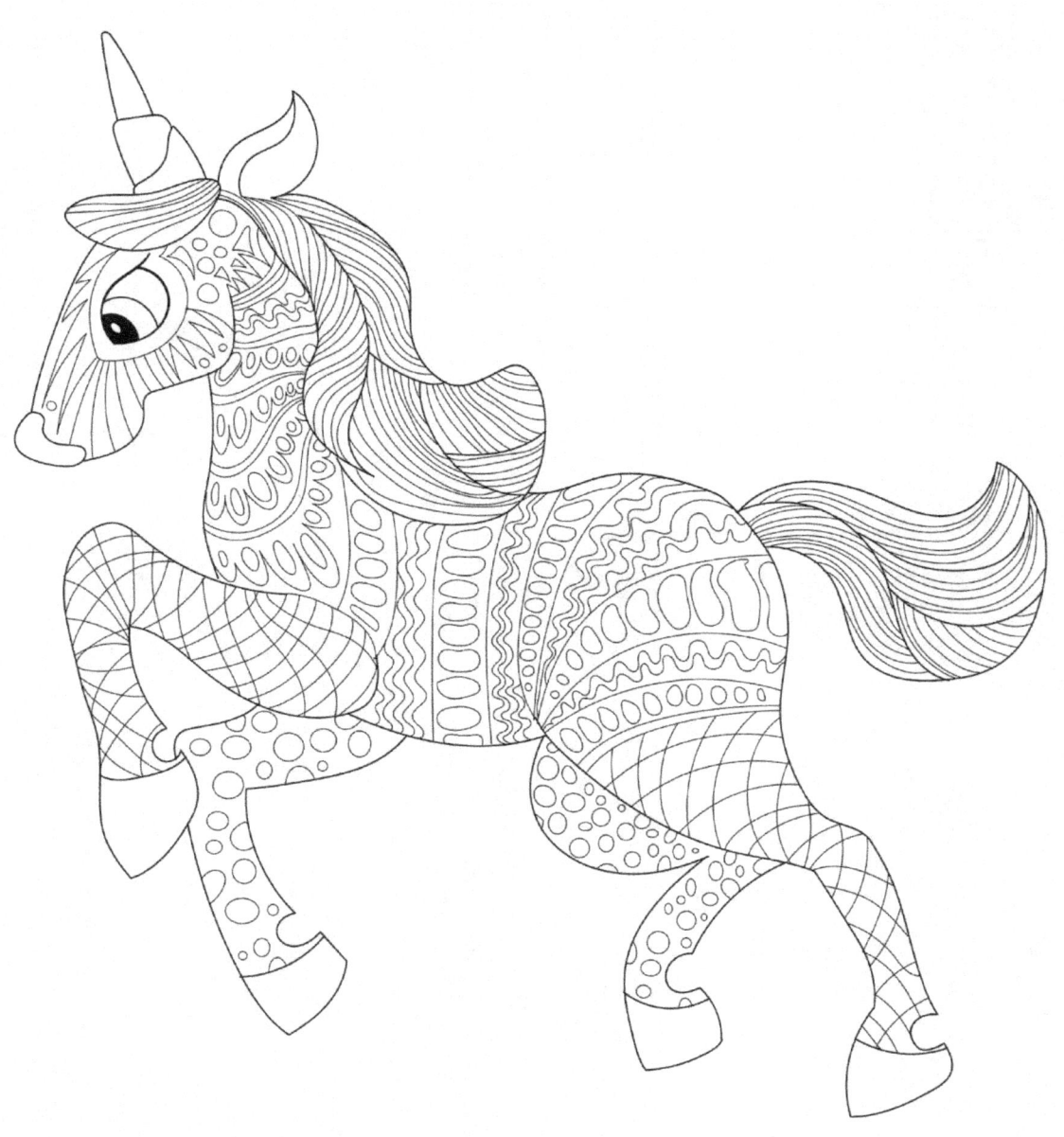

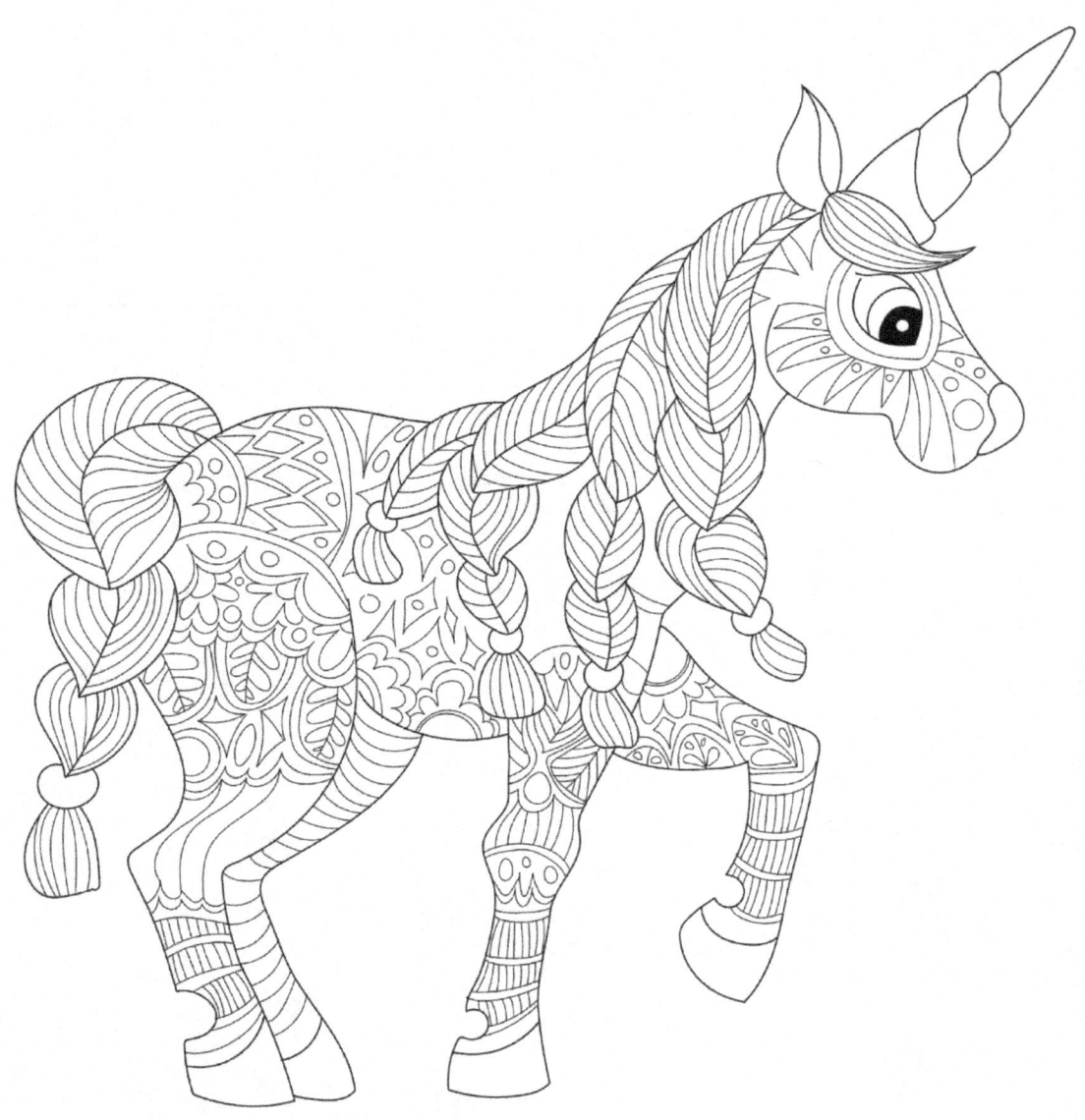

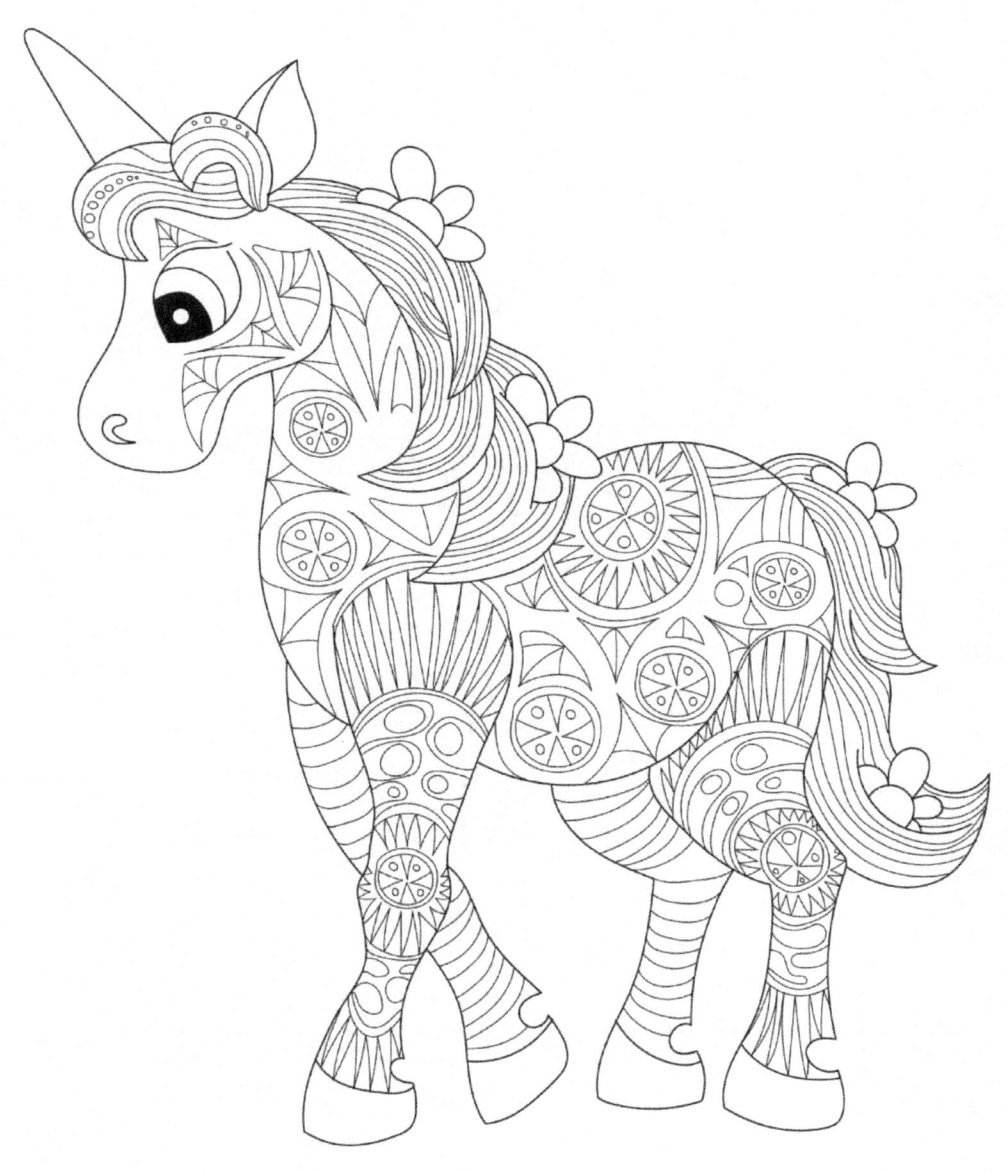

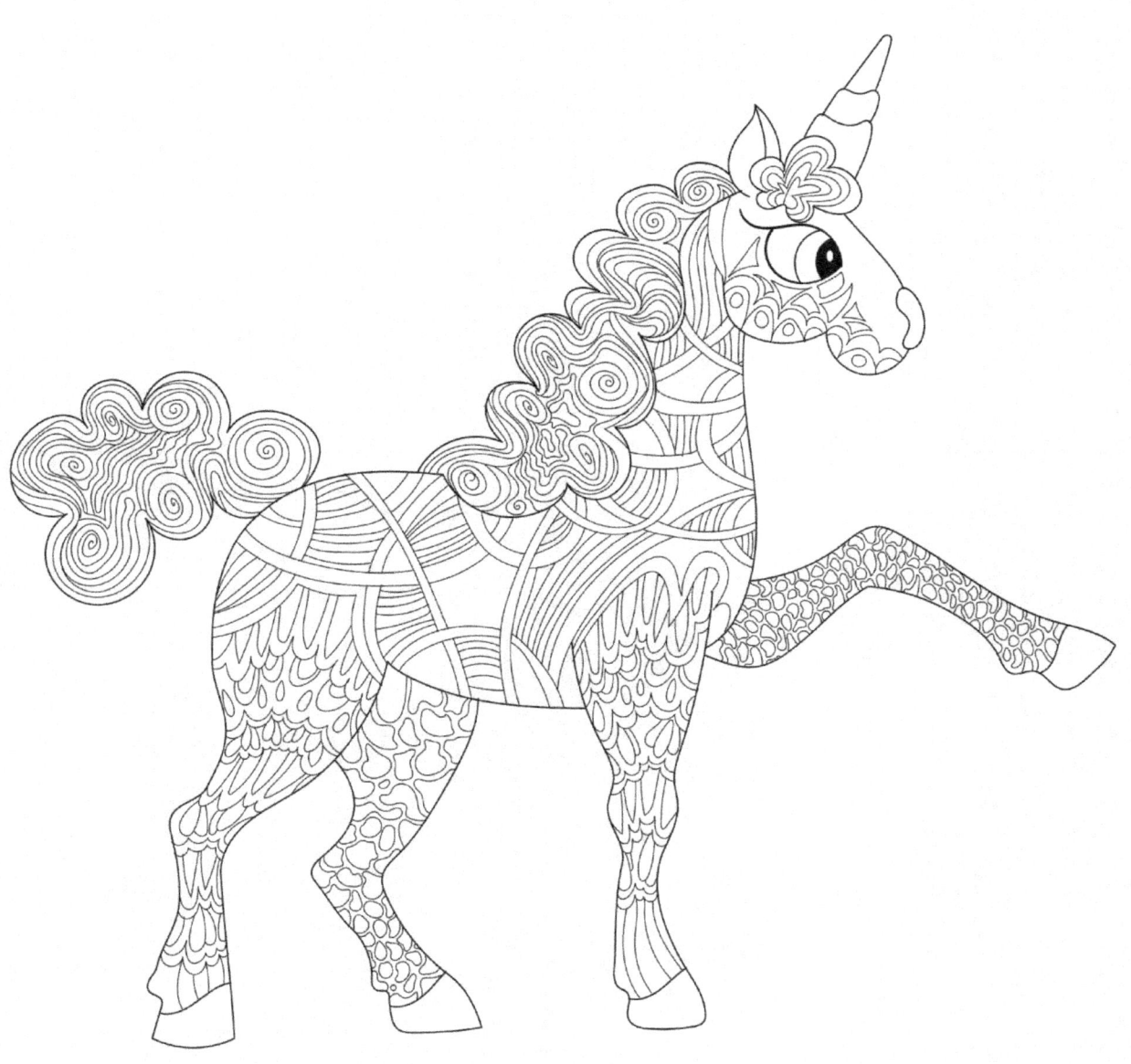

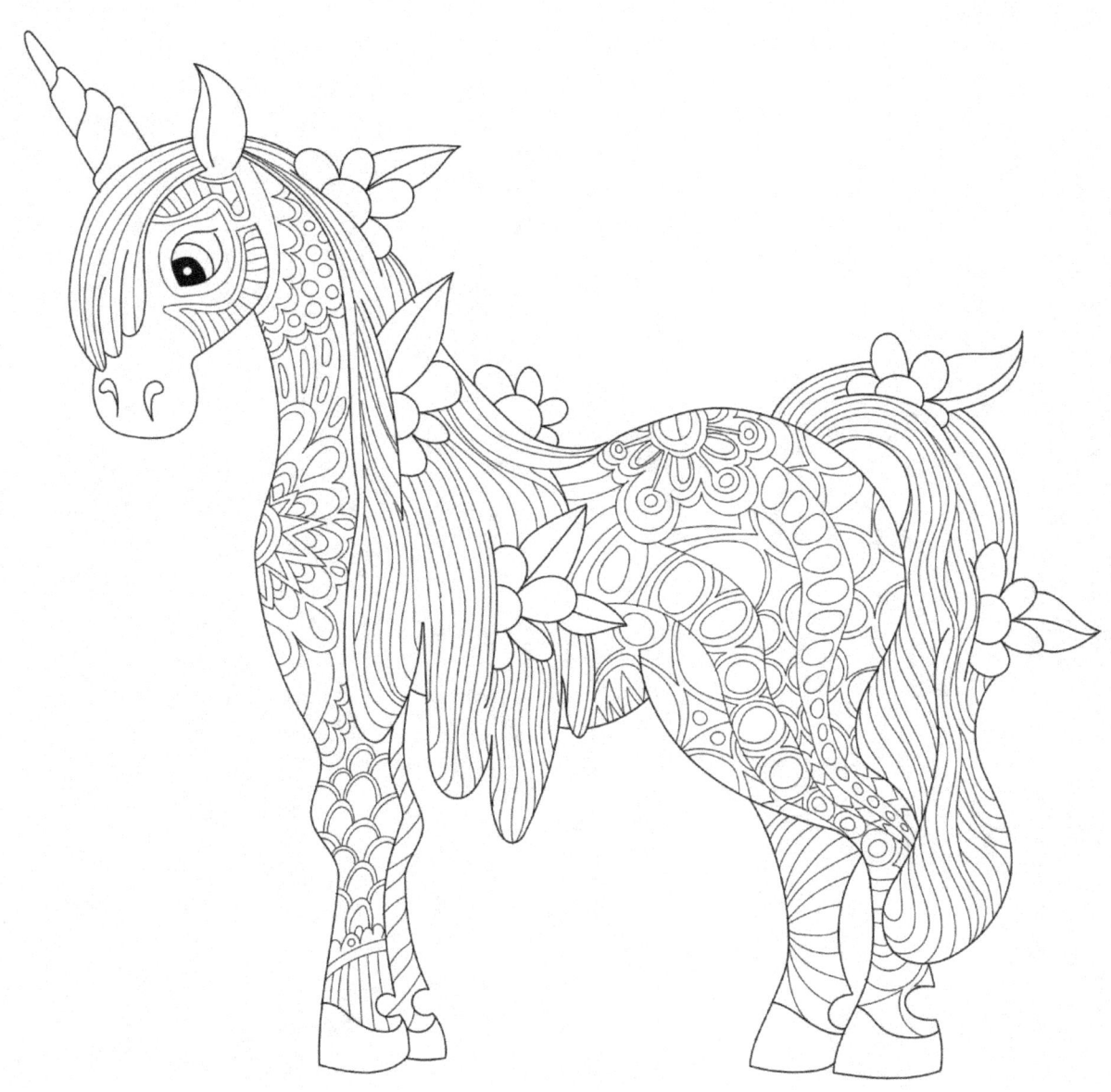

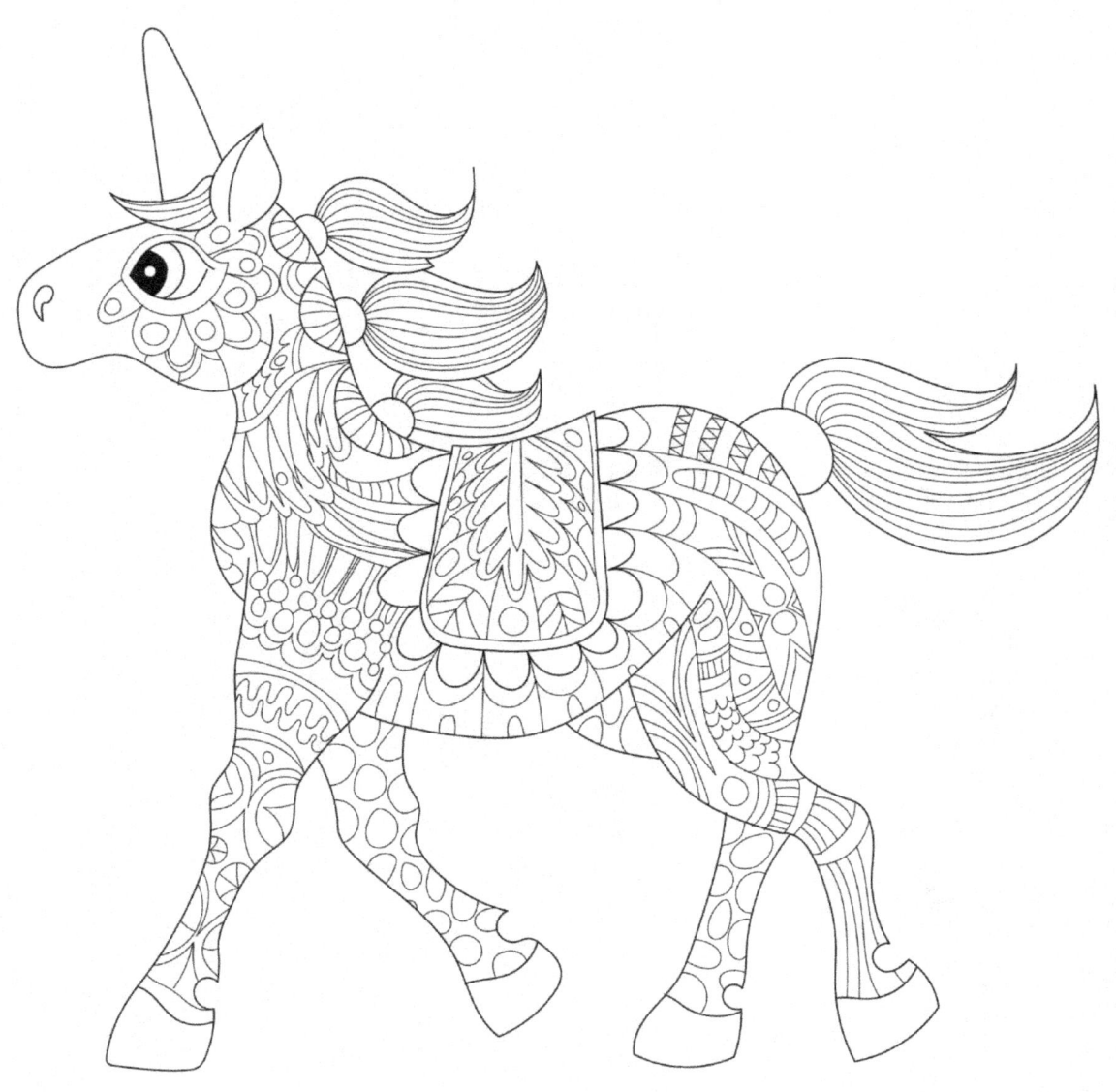

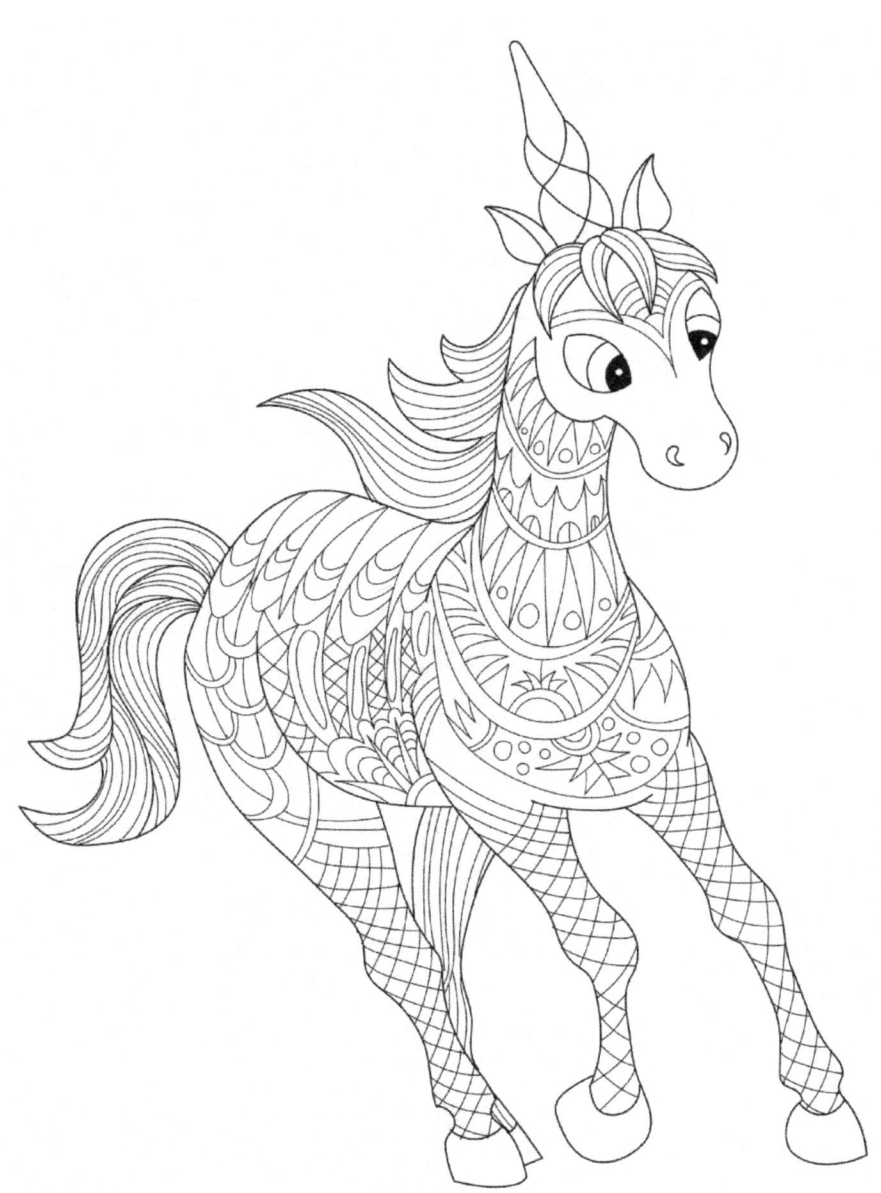

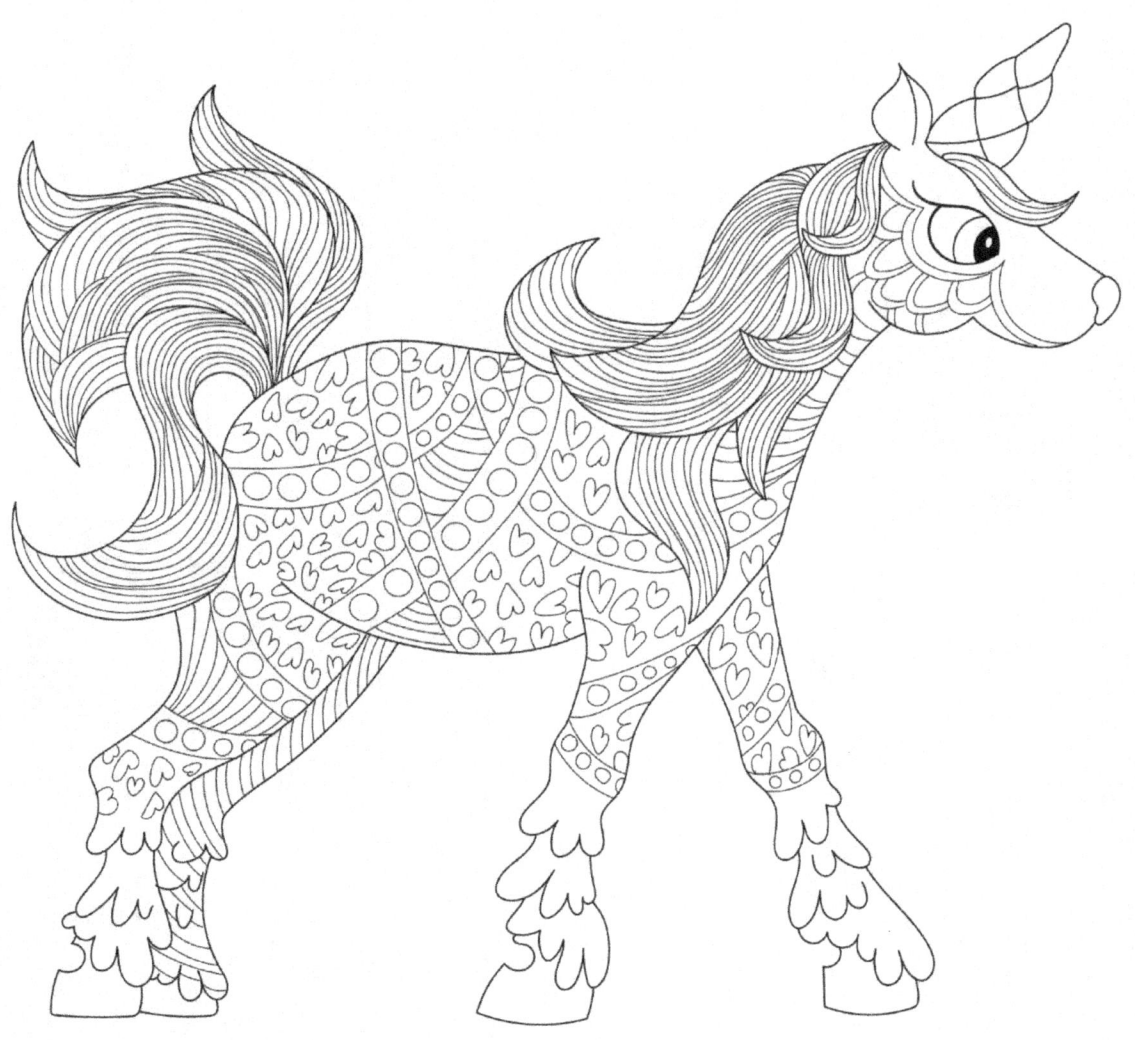

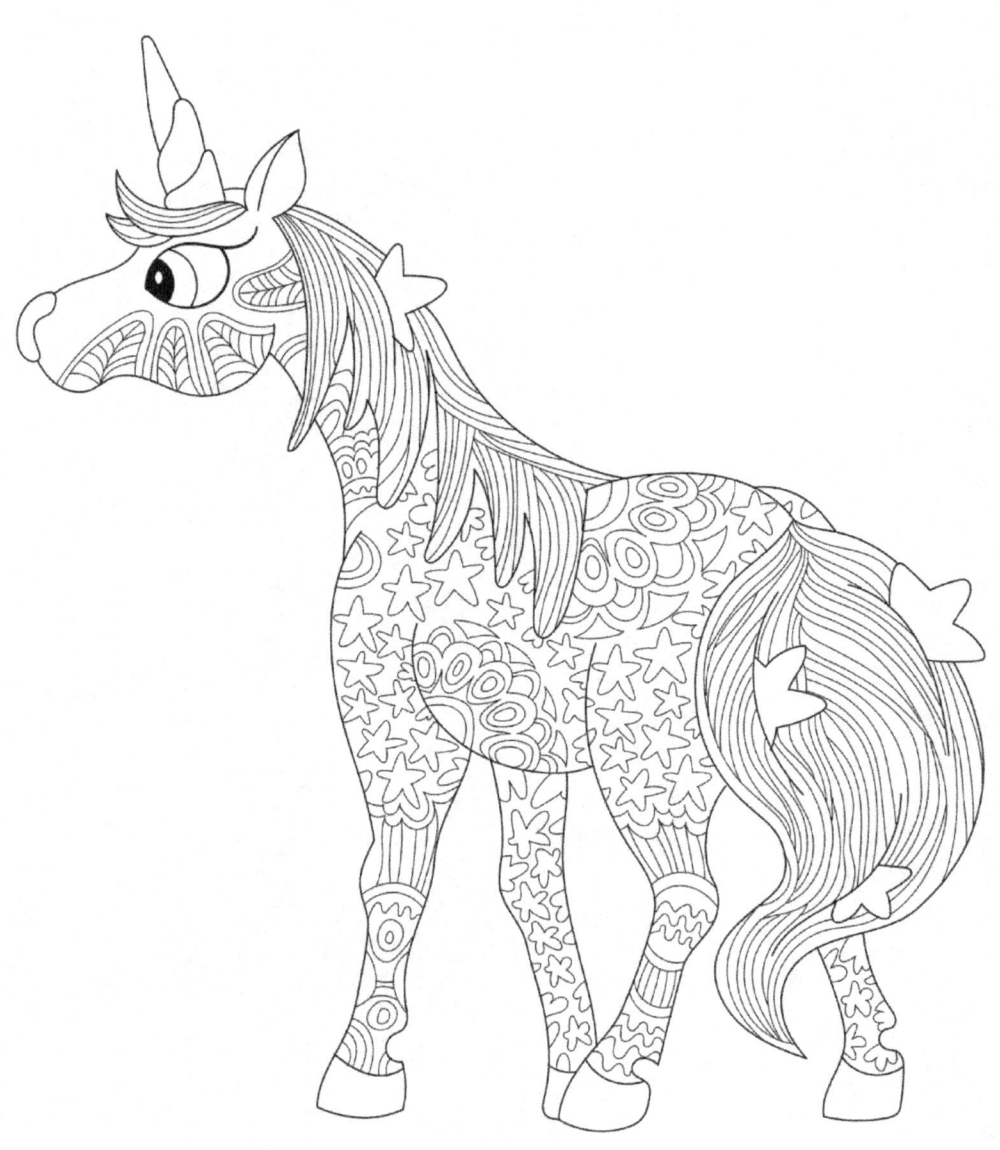

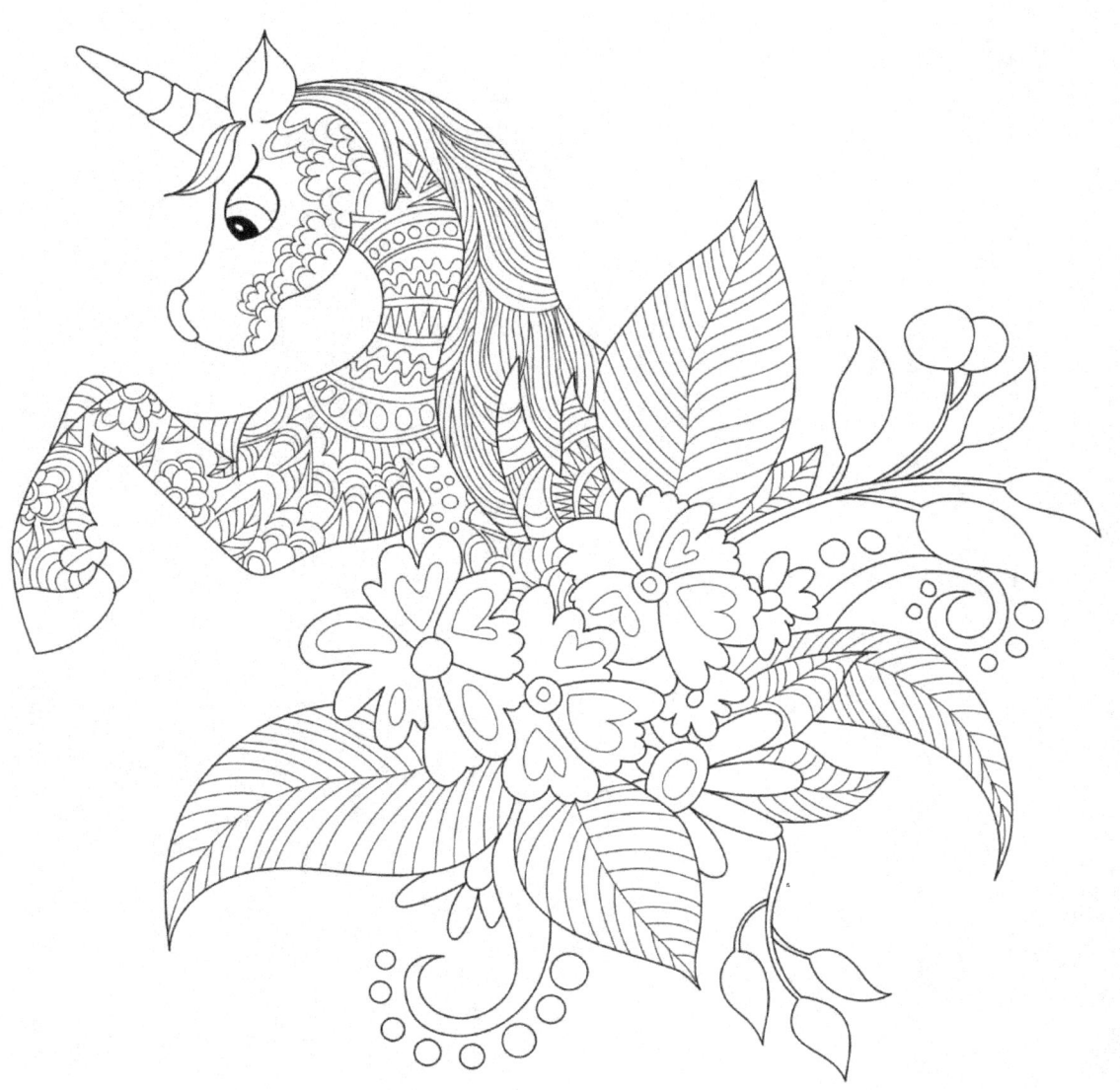

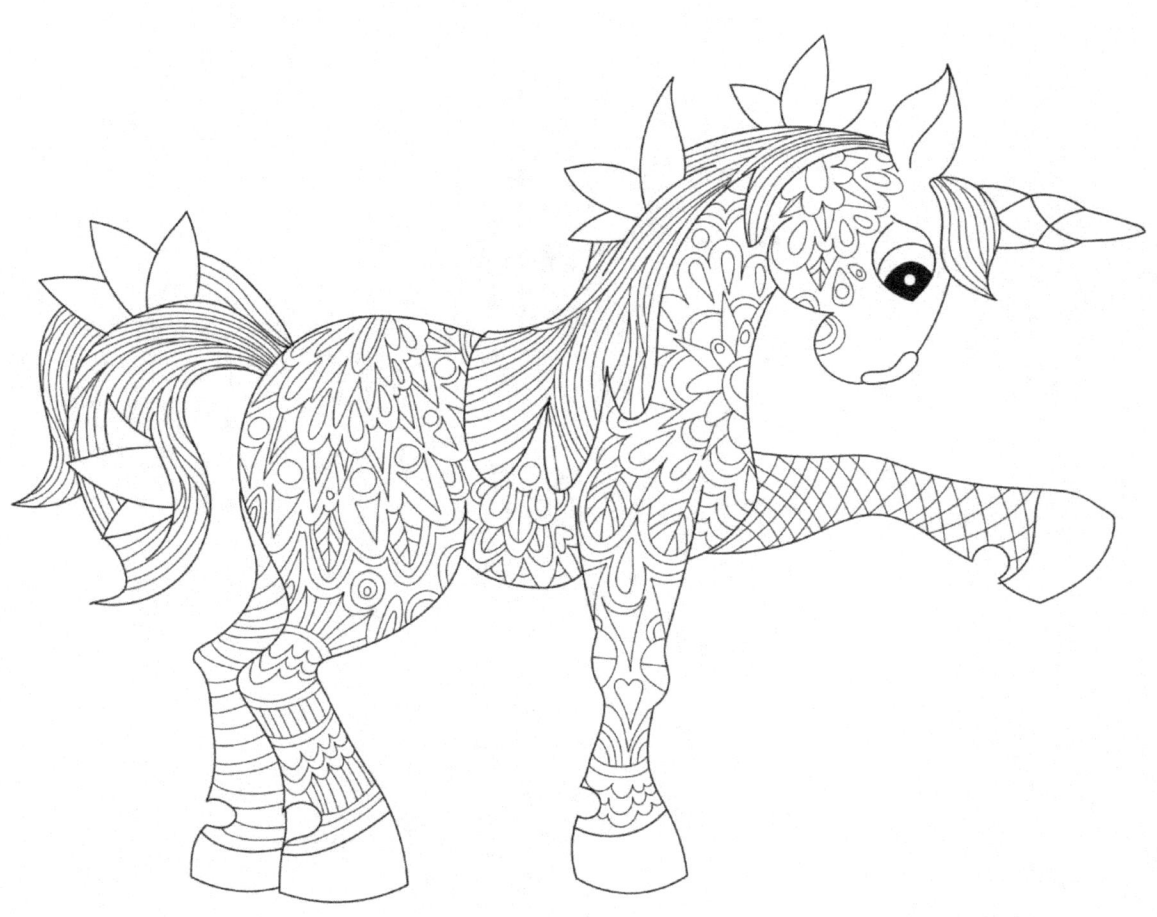

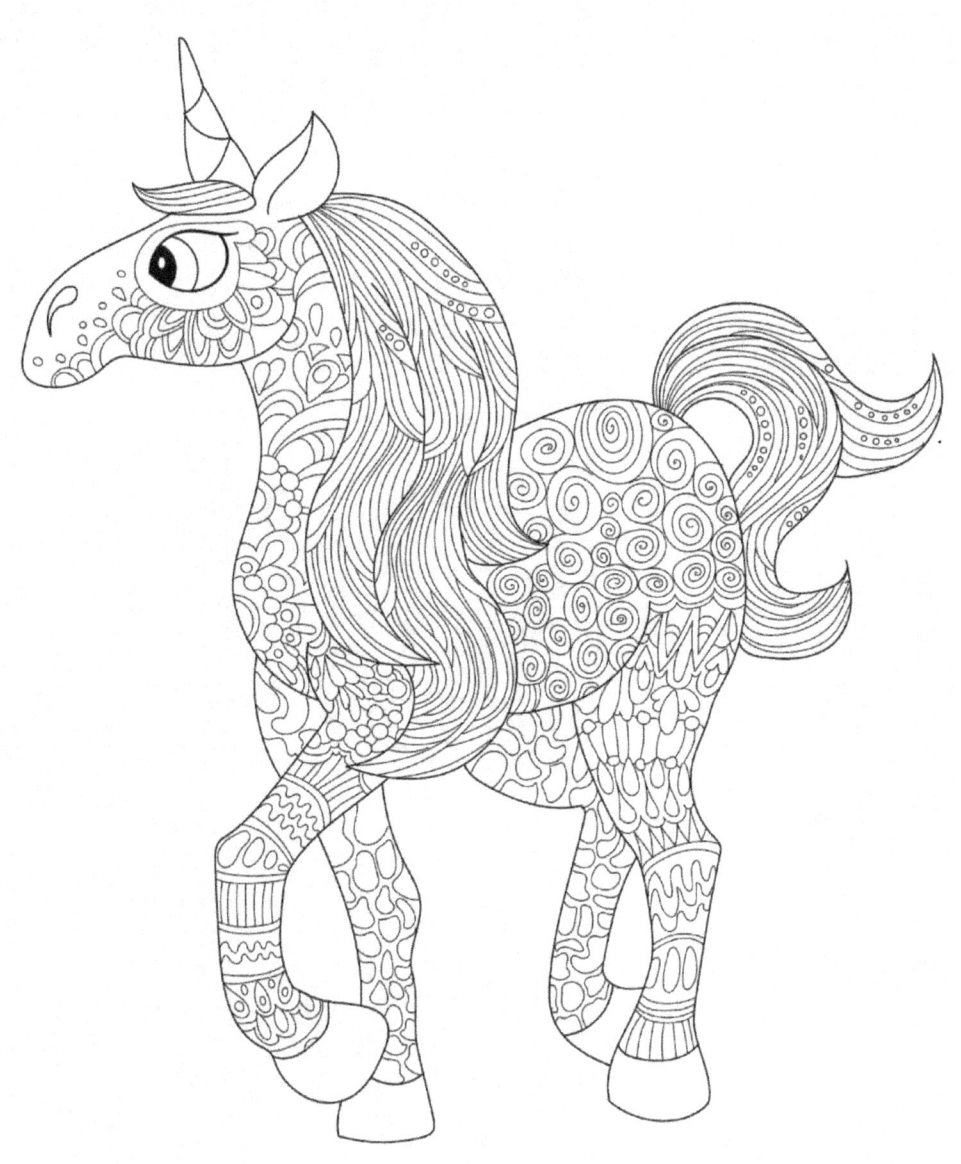

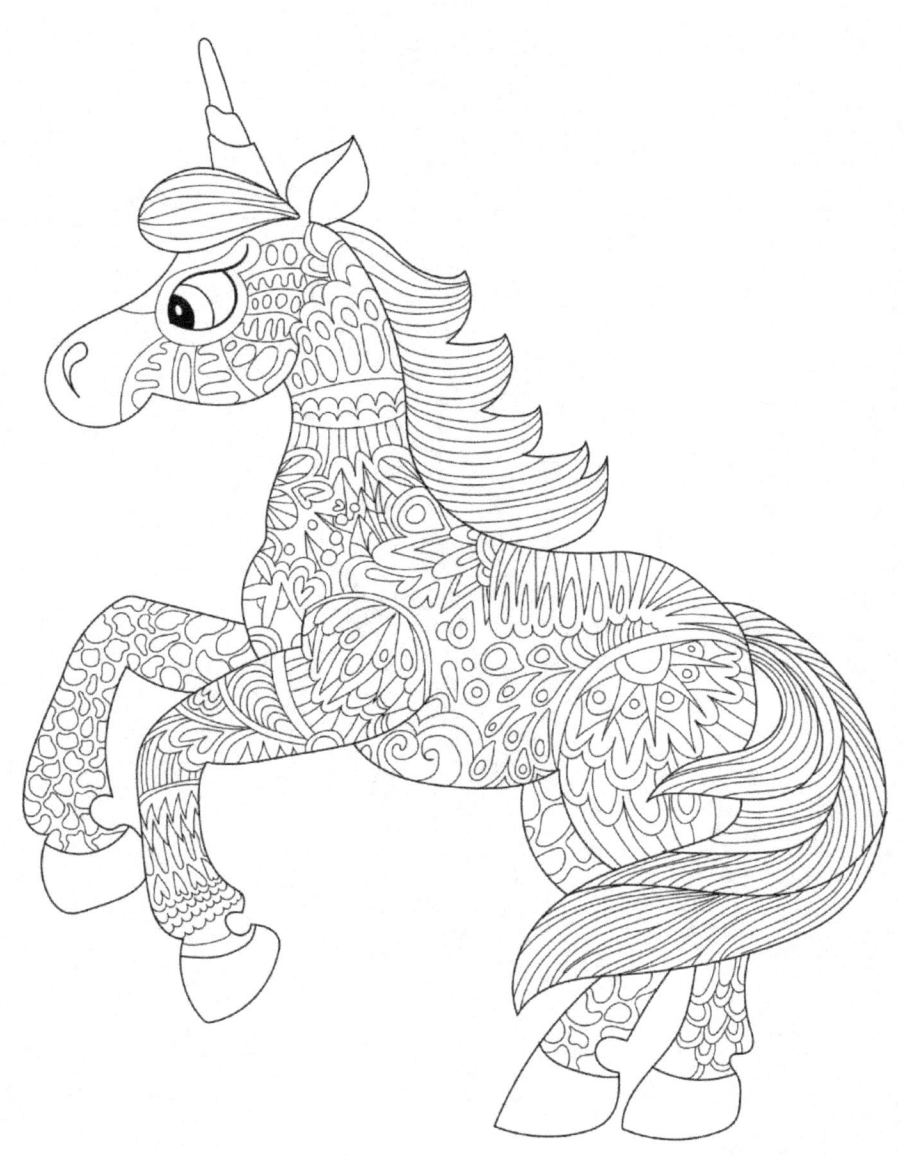

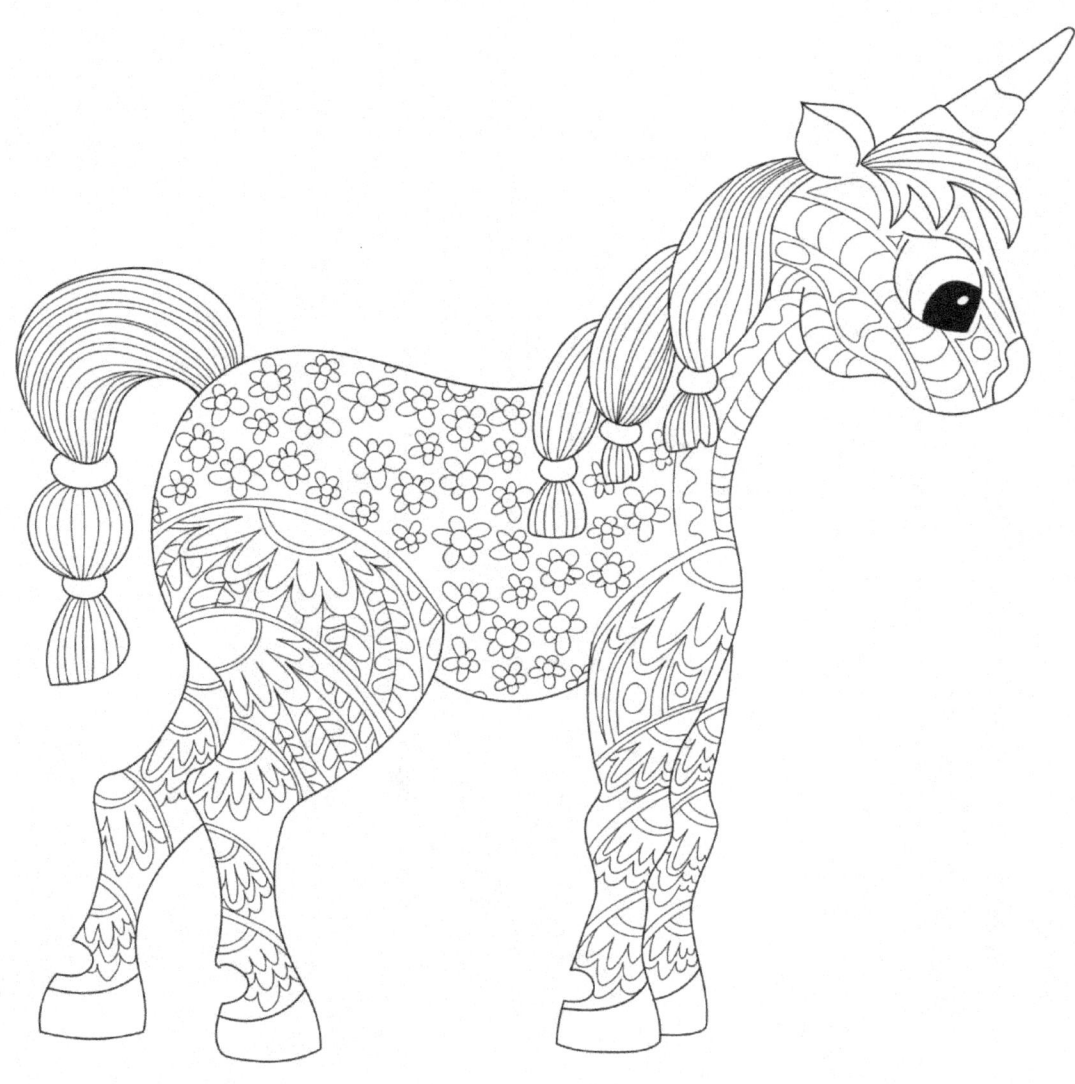

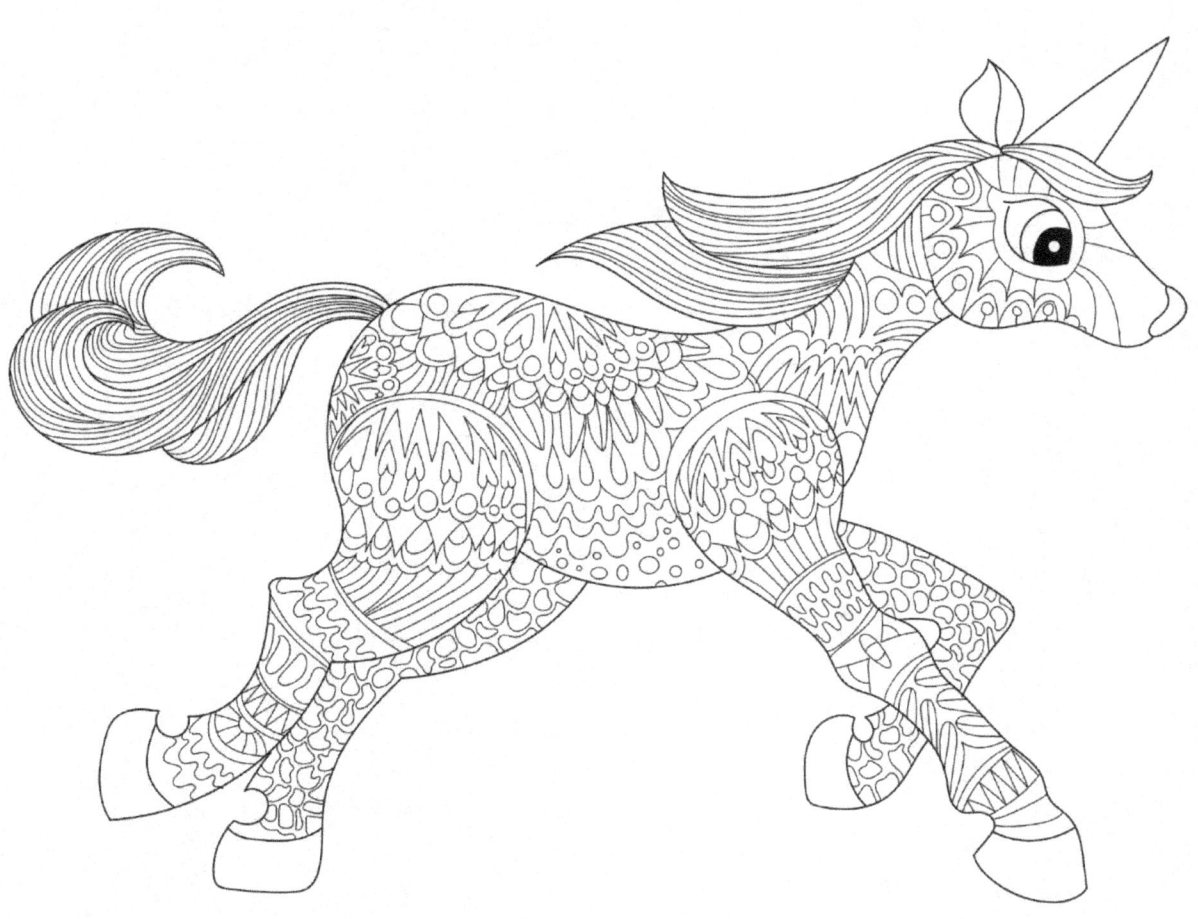

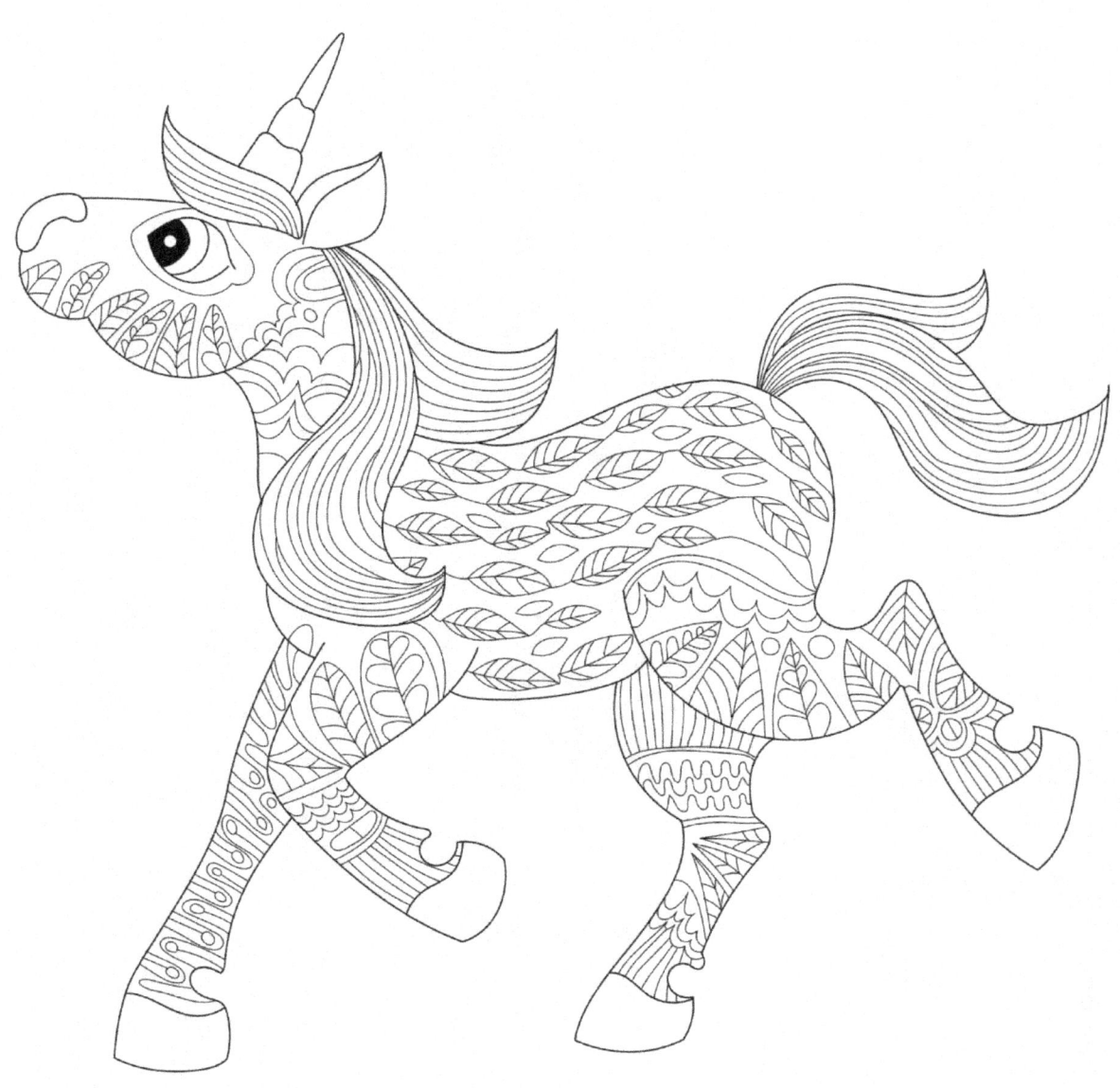

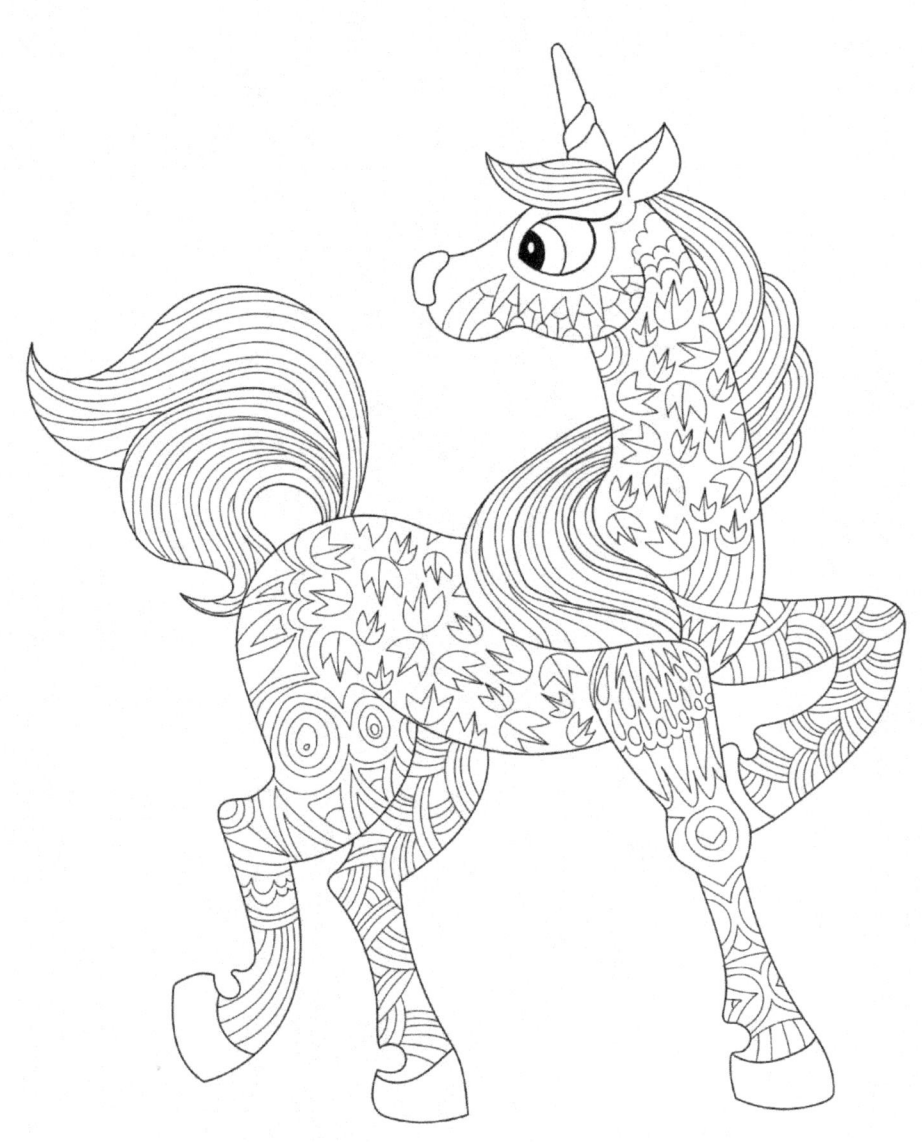

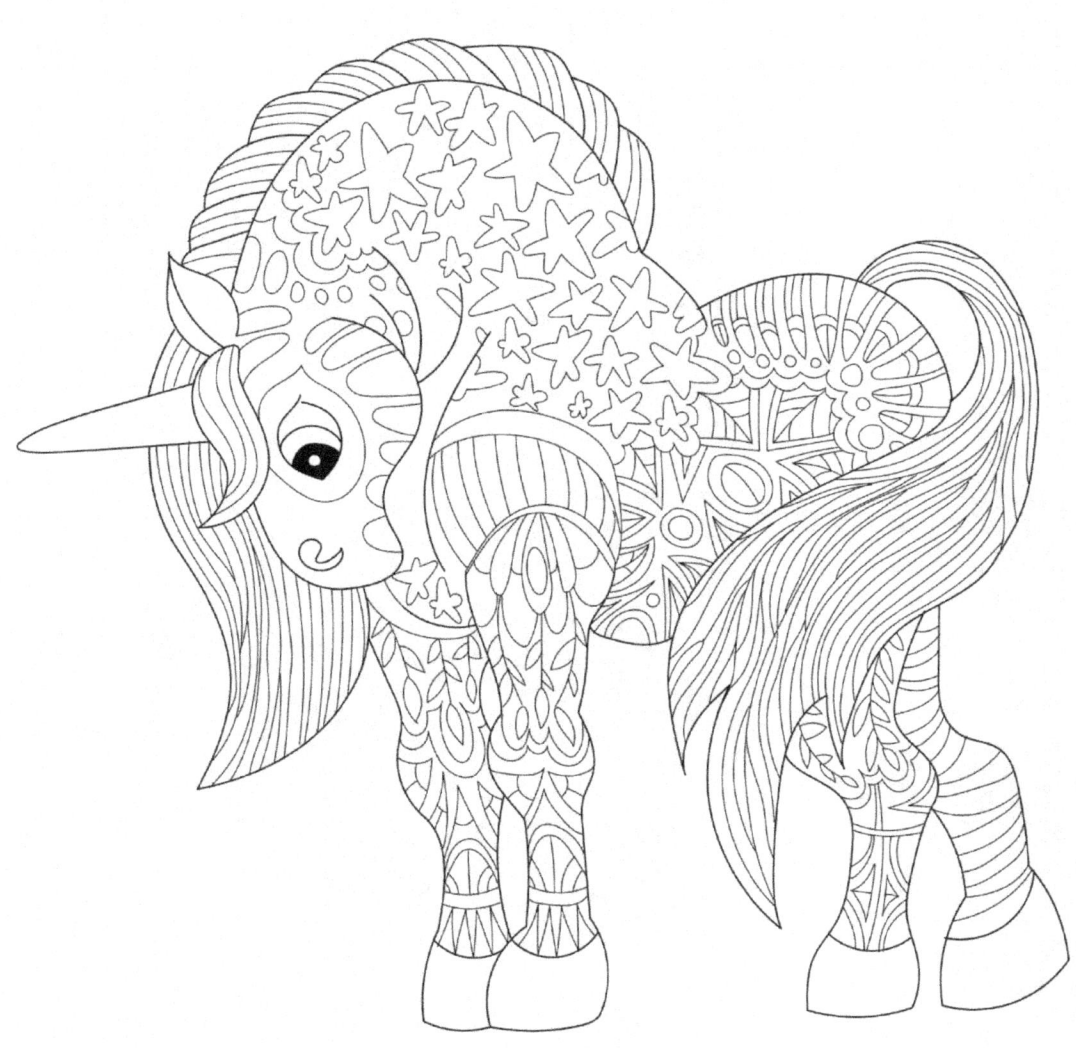

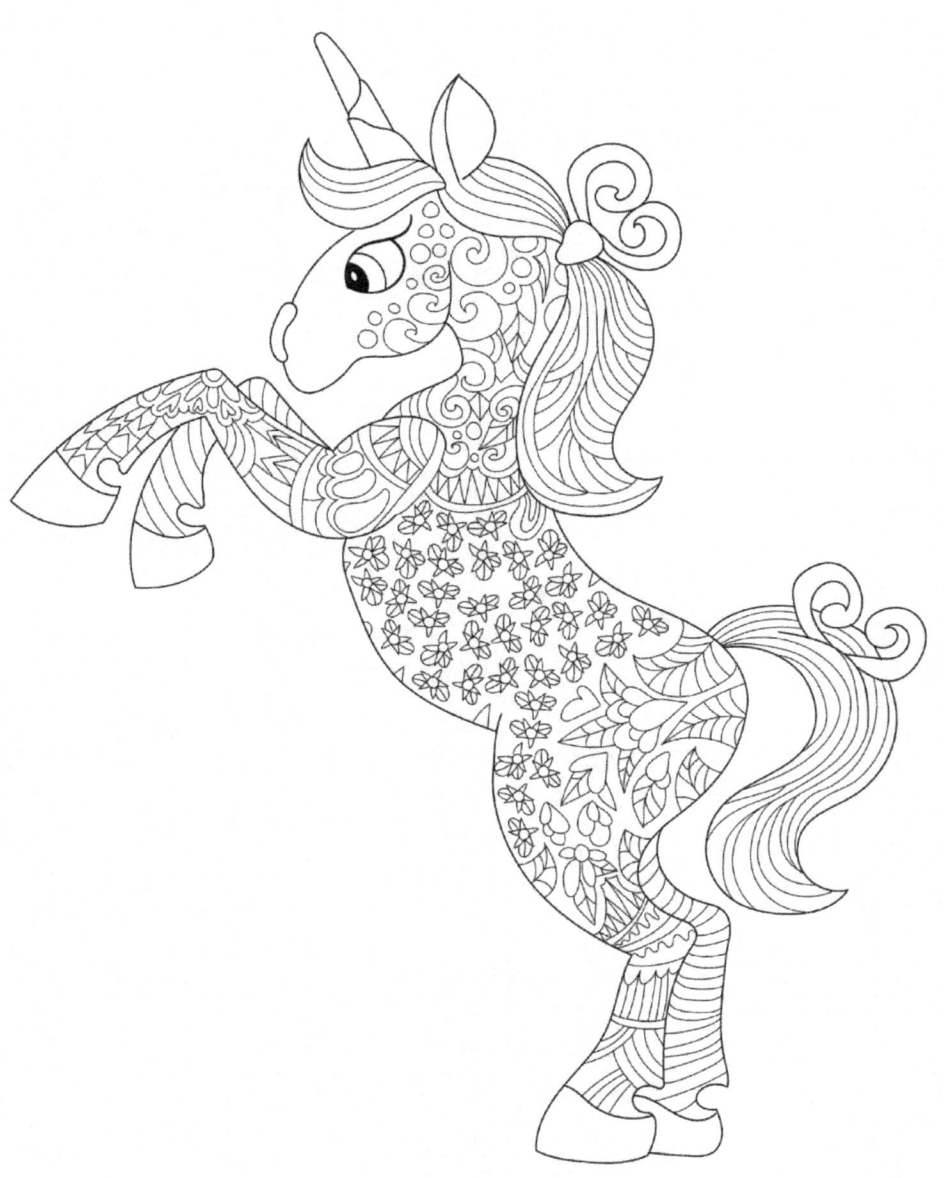

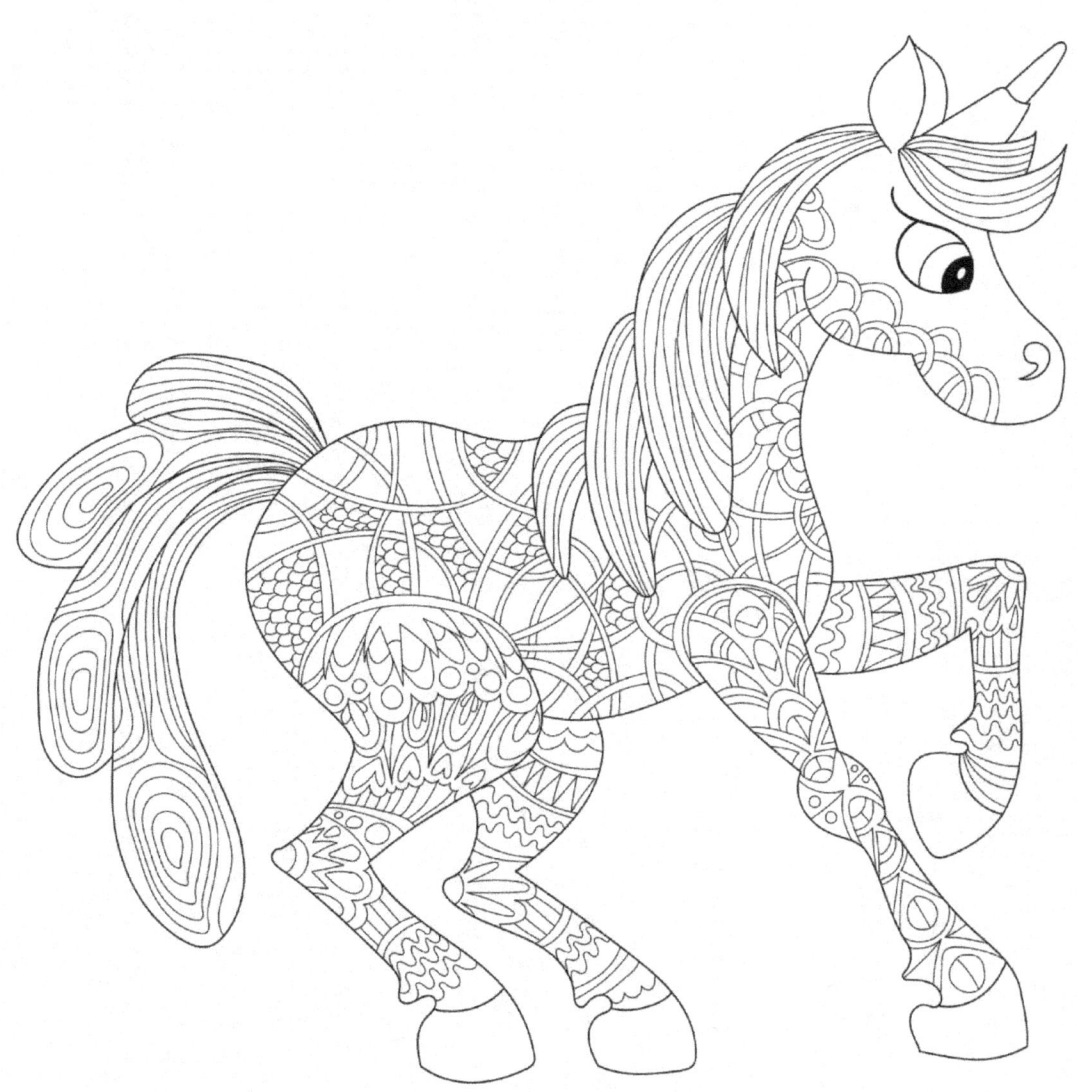

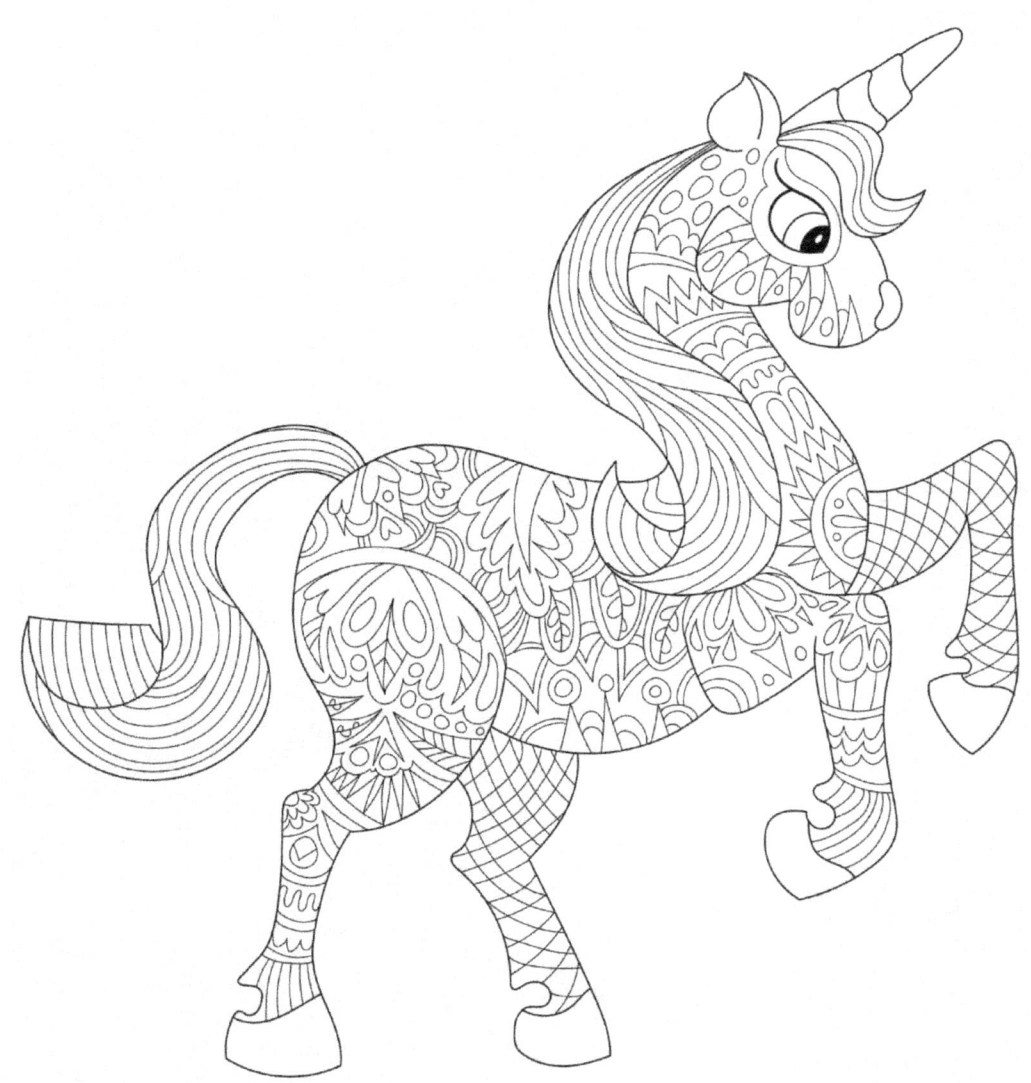

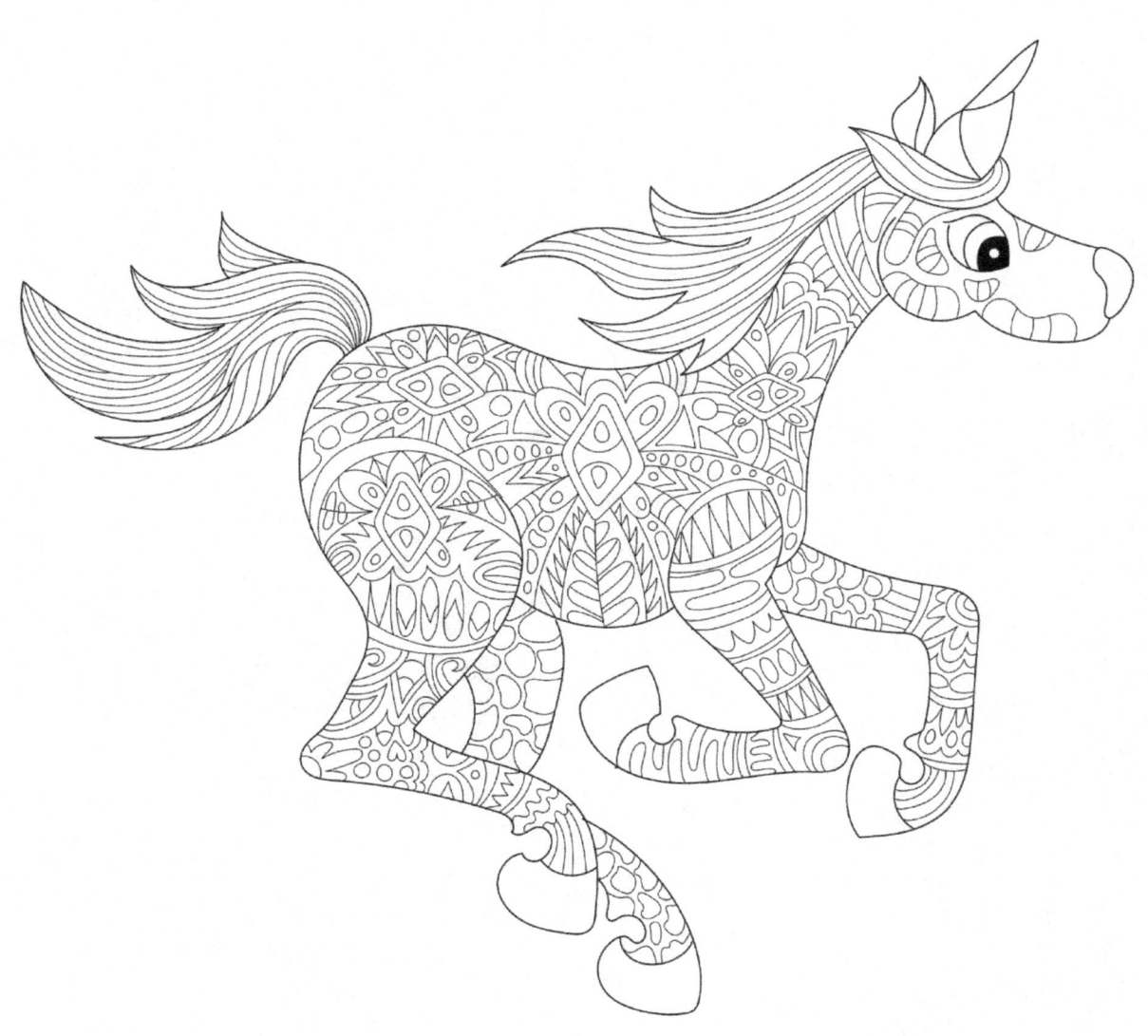

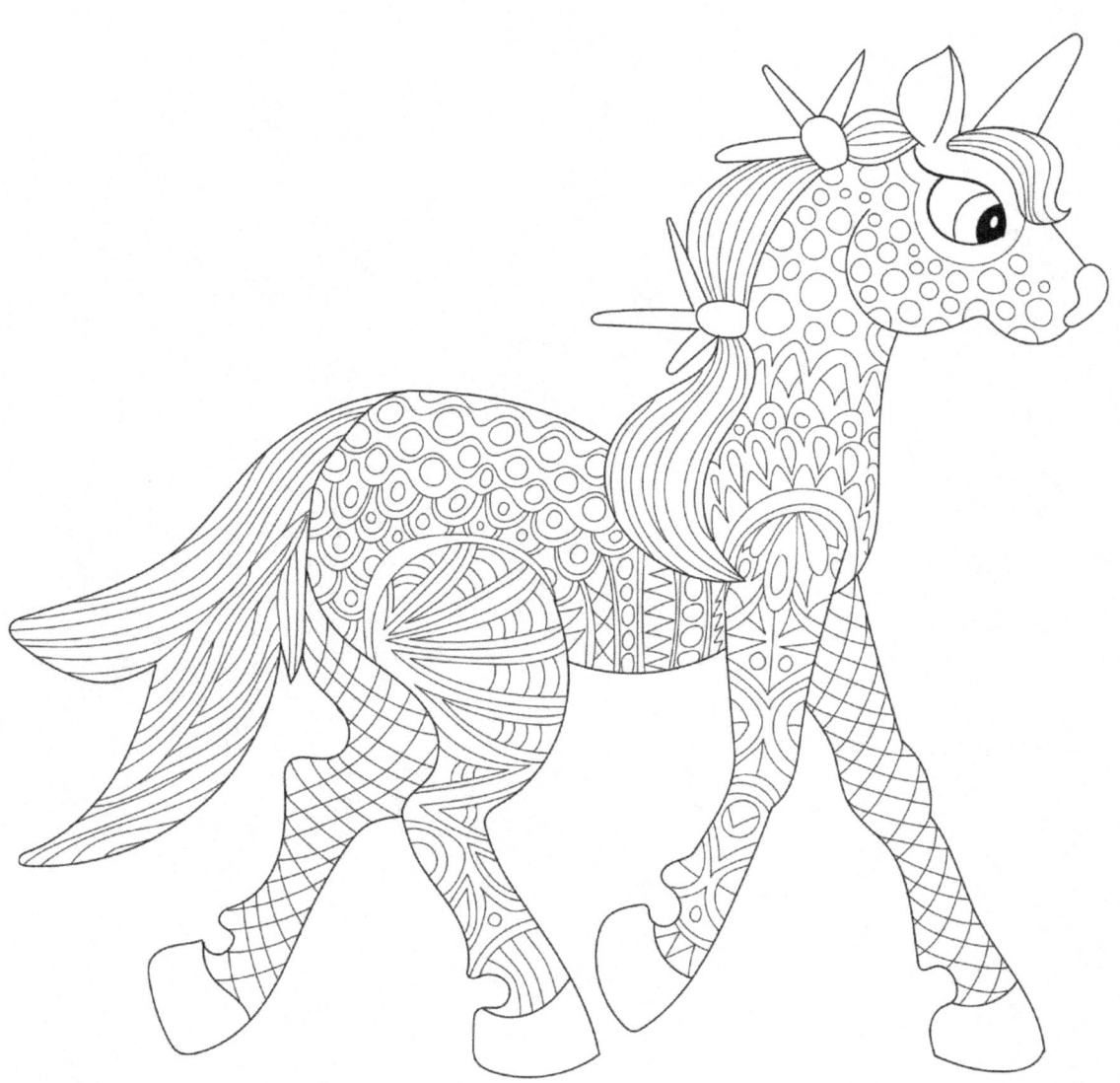

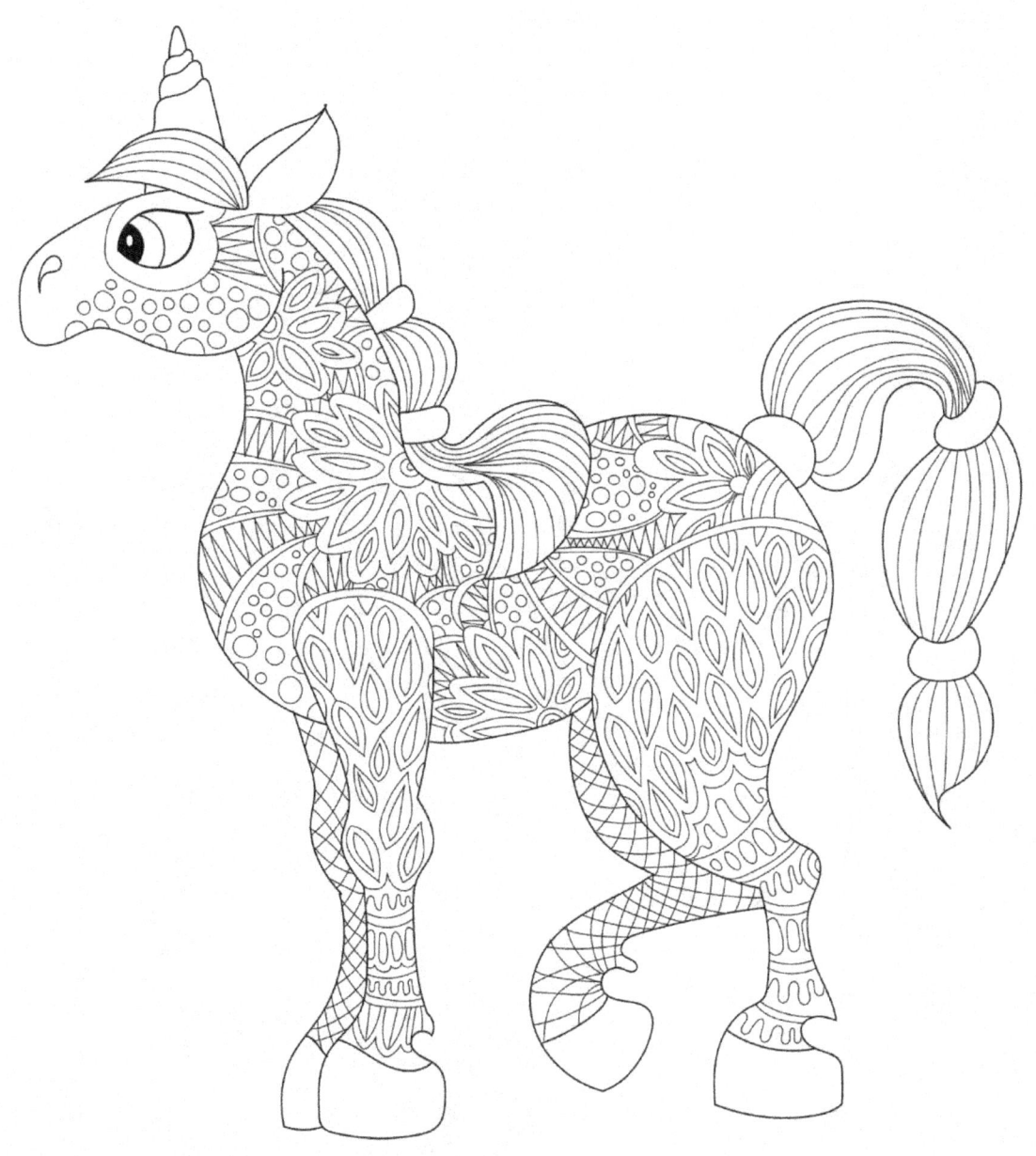

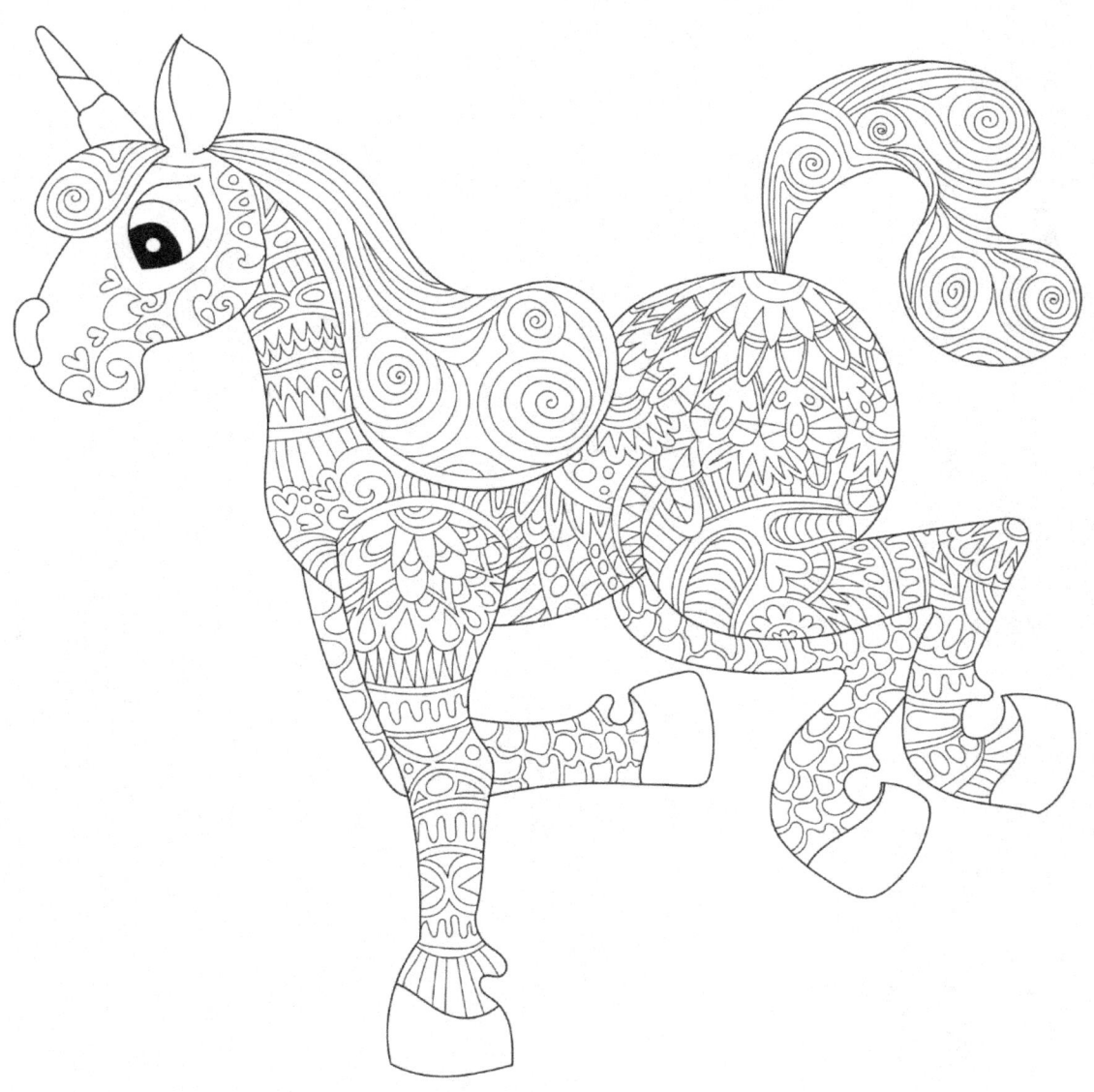

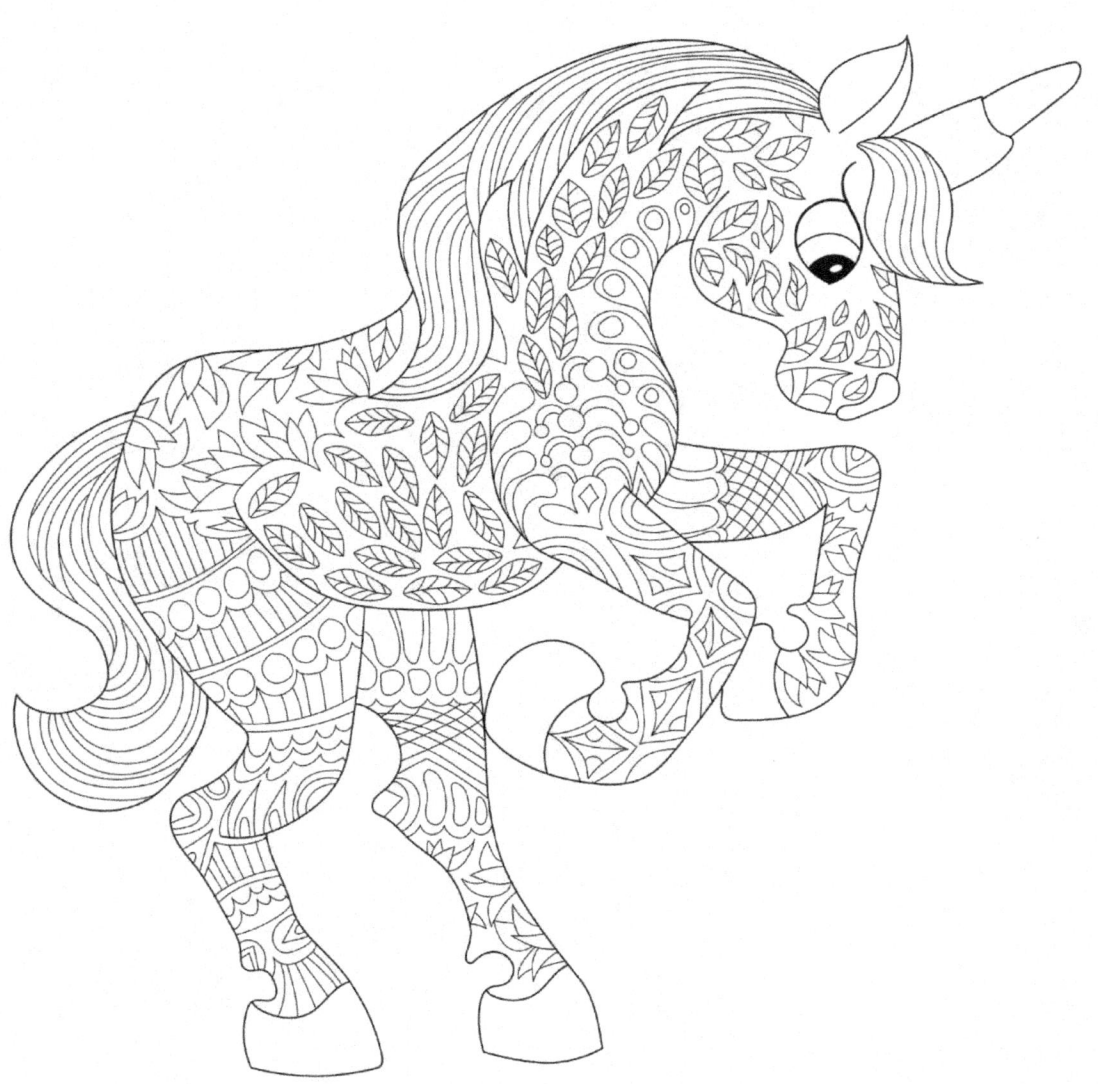

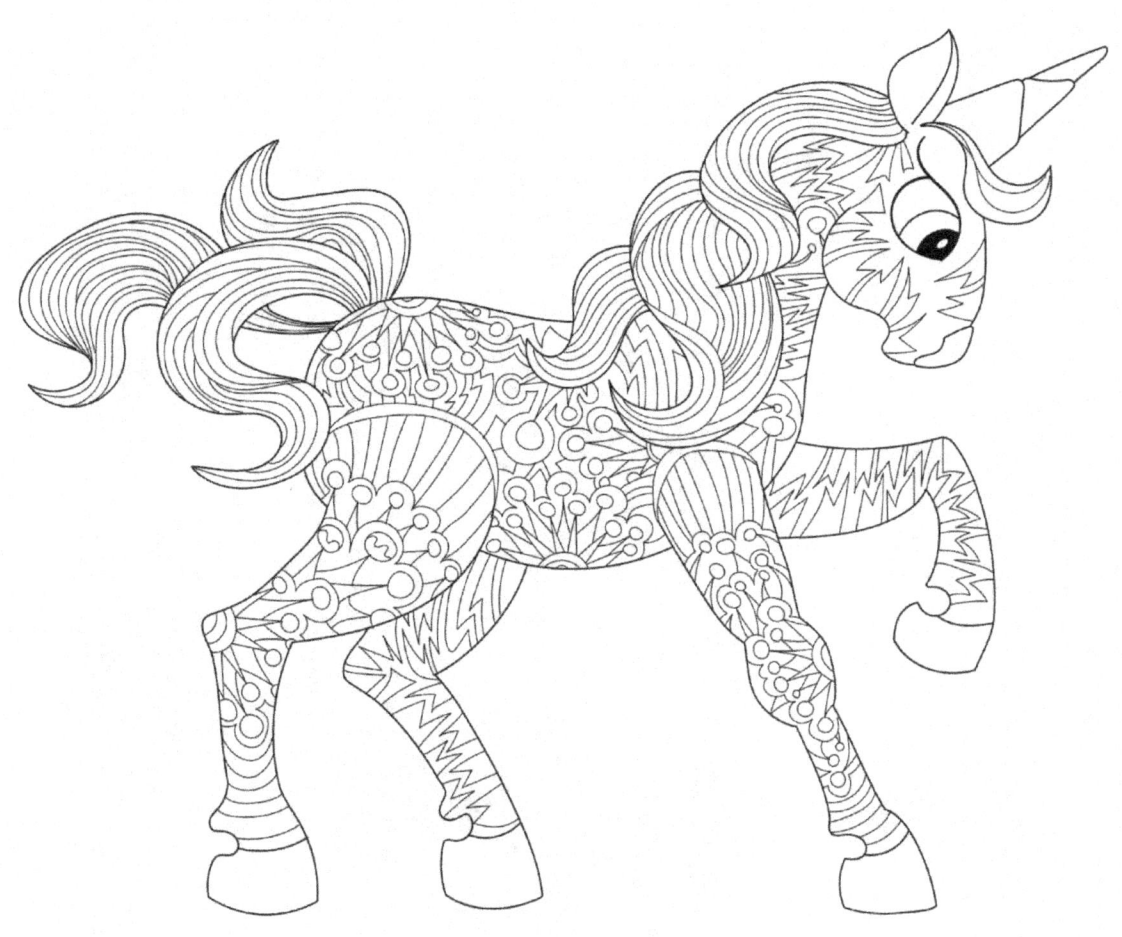

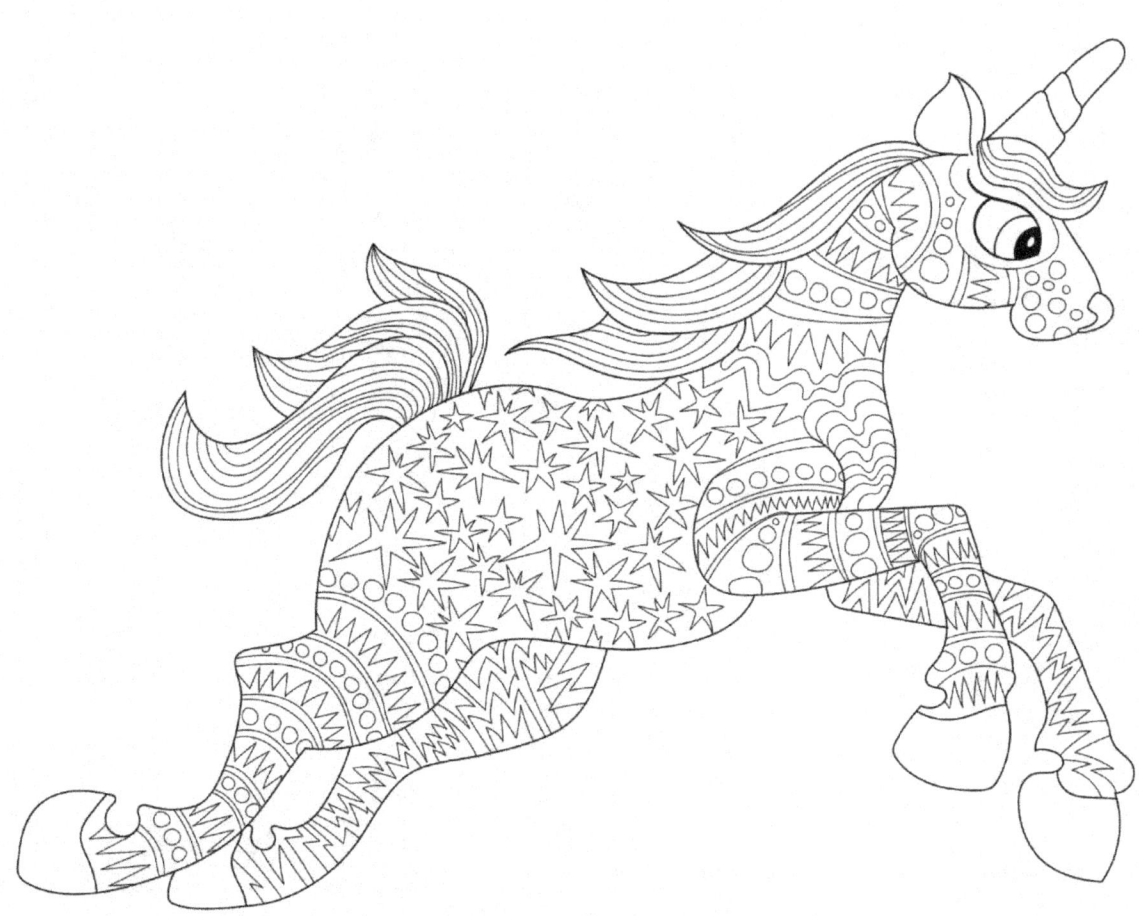

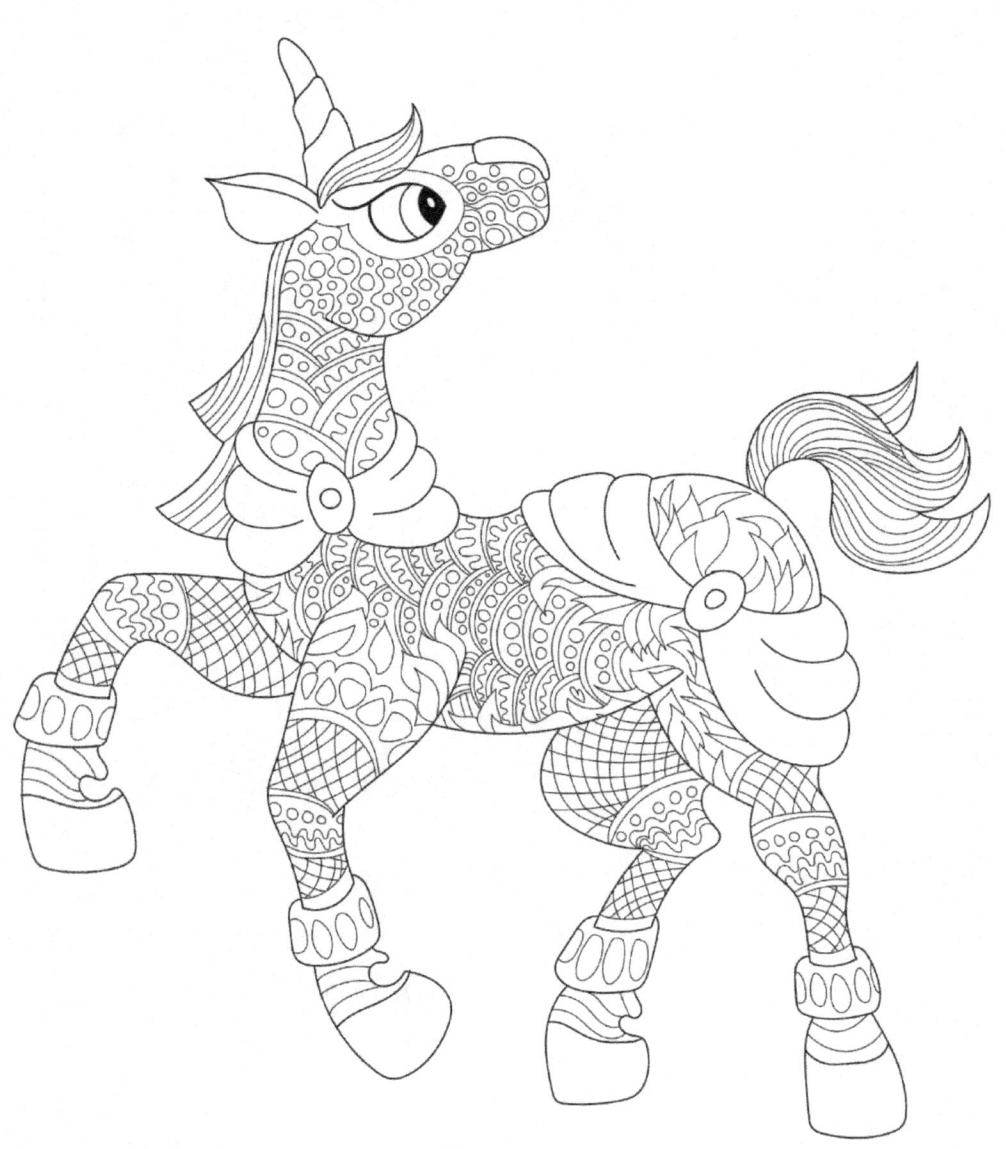

www.ingramcontent.com/pod-product-compliance
Lightning Source LLC
Chambersburg PA
CBHW080837220526
45467CB00008B/2307